Yes, You Can!

This book is dedicated to our children,
Dr. Nafissa Thompson Spires, NaChe' Thompson, and
Stephen Thompson, and our grandsons, Iveren and Isaiah.

Yes, You Can!

Advice for Teachers Who Want a Great Start and a Great Finish With Their Students of Color

Gail L. Thompson

Rufus Thompson

CORWIN
A SAGE Company

CORWIN
A SAGE Company

FOR INFORMATION:

Corwin
A SAGE Company
2455 Teller Road
Thousand Oaks, California 91320
(800) 233-9936
www.corwin.com

SAGE Publications Ltd.
1 Oliver's Yard
55 City Road
London EC1Y 1SP
United Kingdom

SAGE Publications India Pvt. Ltd.
B 1/I 1 Mohan Cooperative Industrial Area
Mathura Road, New Delhi 110 044
India

SAGE Publications Asia-Pacific Pte. Ltd.
3 Church Street
#10-04 Samsung Hub
Singapore 049483

Acquisitions Editor: Dan Alpert
Associate Editor: Kimberly Greenberg
Editorial Assistant: Cesar Reyes
Production Editor: Melanie Birdsall
Copy Editor: Erin Livingston
Typesetter: C&M Digitals (P) Ltd.
Proofreader: Annie Lubinsky
Indexer: Molly Hall
Cover Designer: Candice Harman
Marketing Manager: Stephanie Trkay

Printed in the United States of America

A catalog record of this book is available from the Library of Congress.

ISBN: 978-1-4522-9171-0

This book is printed on acid-free paper.

MIX
Paper from
responsible sources
FSC® C014174

14 15 16 17 18 10 9 8 7 6 5 4 3 2 1

Contents

PART III. Getting Help From the "Village": How to Maximize Your Relations With Parents, Colleagues, and School Leaders

About the Authors

The authors of *Yes, You Can!* have nearly 60 years of combined teaching experience and are the parents of three adult children, including two educators.

Dr. Gail L. Thompson, the Wells Fargo Endowed Professor of Education at Fayetteville State University in North Carolina and the recipient of Claremont Graduate University's Distinguished Alumna Award, has written numerous books, including the critically acclaimed *Through Ebony Eyes: What Teachers Need to Know but Are Afraid to Ask About African American Students* and *The Power of One: How You Can Help or Harm African American Students,* which was nominated for the National Staff Development Council's Book of the Year award. Dr. Thompson, who taught junior high and high school for 14 years, has given keynote addresses and conducted professional development workshops for educators and K–12 students at conferences and schools and has conducted parent empowerment workshops at churches and schools throughout the United States. She has also appeared on numerous radio and television programs, and her essays and articles have been published in newspapers and academic journals.

Dr. Thompson's coauthor and husband, **Rufus Thompson,** wrote part of the Heath (now Houghton Mifflin) Middle Level Literature series and High School Anthology. Starting in 1988, he trained teachers throughout California on how to implement technology into the curriculum using best practices and sound classroom principles and taught middle school for 17 years before becoming the technology coordinator of the Mountain View School District in Ontario, California. He also served as a representative on the San Bernardino County BestNet Advisory Board to Superintendents, and his Middle School Journalism program was recognized by the National Middle School Association as one of 80 innovative programs in the United States. Mr. Thompson, who has a master's degree, has taught courses at the University of Redlands, Chapman University (under contract with Webmedia Solutions), Claremont Graduate

University, and California Polytechnic University, Pomona as an adjunct. He has also provided extensive professional development workshops for teachers and school administrators, organized conferences, and given presentations at several conferences, including the National School Board Association, the National Middle School Association, Computer Using Education (CUE), and California Educational Technology Professional Association (CETPA). Mr. Thompson recently retired and is the owner of Tech Guy in a Box, a technology and best-practices consulting company.

Acknowledgments

From Gail: I thank God for giving me the idea, motivation, and strength to cocreate this book project. I am grateful to my husband, Rufus, for his hard work and contributions; to my children, Dr. Nafissa Thompson Spires, NaChe' Thompson, and Stephen Thompson for their ongoing encouragement; and to my grandsons, Iveren and Isaiah, for bringing so much joy and laughter into my life. My assistant, Ms. Angela Davis, proofread the first three chapters and provided positive feedback. I also want to thank all of the individuals who encouraged Rufus and me to complete this project, and I am extremely grateful to the educators who completed the Teacher Confidence (TC) Study questionnaire. Dan Alpert is a wonderful editor and is delightful to work with. Thank you, Dan, for believing in this project and for your ongoing support. Along with Rufus, I also want to thank Dr. Randall Lindsey, Dr. Angela Louque, and Lane Rankin, the founder and CEO of Illuminate Education, for their wonderful endorsements for this book, and Dr. Jenny Rankin for her enthusiasm and words of encouragement about this book.

From Rufus: I thank God for my wife, Gail, and our children and for the opportunity to collaborate on this book. I would also like to thank my colleagues and friends who, throughout the years, have provided support for my ideas, goals, and policies that made educating students easy and exciting. I am extremely grateful to Yvette Coria, my former assistant, for giving me permission to use the parent scripts that she created.

Publisher's Acknowledgments: Corwin gratefully acknowledges the contributions of the following reviewers:

Lori Helman
Associate Professor University of Minnesota

Fernando Nunez
Principal Isaac School District #5
Phoenix, AZ

Joy Pearson
Project Facilitator Employee Onboarding & Development Department
Clark County School District
Las Vegas, NV

Josán Perales
Teacher Vista Grande High School
Taos, NM

Peggy Deal Redman
Professor of Education
La Fetra Family Endowed Chair for Excellence in Teaching and Service
University of La Verne

A. Rogers
Educational Consultant
Tucson, AZ

Introduction

At some point in their career, many teachers—especially beginning teachers—have either said "I quit!" or wished that they could quit teaching and do something else. Most began teaching with high hopes of helping children and having a rewarding career, but soon they became disappointed. In fact, according to a recently published national study, teacher morale is currently at a 20-year all-time low.[1] Decreases in education funding, massive teacher layoffs, pressures to improve standardized test scores, and the disconnect from parents and even from students that many teachers feel have increased the challenges that teachers face. Consequently, being a teacher is tougher than ever—especially in urban and low-income schools—and these circumstances drive many teachers to consider quitting or to actually quit.

Obviously, if you are a teacher who is feeling disappointed, disillusioned, or who has thought about quitting, what you need is a way to stay motivated, encouraged, and to persist, even when circumstances look bleak. *Yes, You Can! Advice for Teachers Who Want a Great Start and a Great Finish With Their Students of Color* will help you do this and will also help you excel at teaching. Although our main goal is to empower beginning teachers, *all* teachers can benefit from the wealth of information in *Yes, You Can!*

This reader-friendly book contains original research based on the Teacher Confidence (TC) Study, which I (Dr. Gail L. Thompson) conducted as well as practical strategies and advice, true stories, professional development exercises, and recommended readings that will empower you. The TC Study will provide you with important feedback from 293 teacher interns, beginning teachers, and veteran teachers regarding a variety of topics, including classroom management; working with students from socioeconomically, racially, and ethnically diverse backgrounds; working with parents; working with struggling students; working with high achievers; and handling racial and ethnic conflicts.

ABOUT THE BOOK'S ORGANIZATION

Each chapter begins with one or more true stories and related exercises for you to complete, followed by chapter highlights, results from the TC Study, additional exercises, practical advice and strategies, and a final professional growth activity. **Part I, Do You *Really* Love *All of Them*? Assessing Your Teaching Self-Confidence About Working With Various Types of Students,** is designed to help you better understand your beliefs about fairness, income, and gender and how these beliefs pertain to effective teaching. In the three chapters in this section, you will learn why self-confidence plays a crucial role in your teaching efficacy, discover the connection between fear and self-confidence, examine what the TC Study participants said about their teaching self-confidence, compare and contrast your beliefs and teaching self-confidence with the study participants' comments and self-ratings, and learn practical strategies to increase your teaching self-confidence.

The three chapters in **Part II, Student Empowerment–Teacher Empowerment: Increasing Your Teaching Self-Confidence and Your Teaching Efficacy,** contain research-based practical instructional strategies that will help you increase your effectiveness with all students but particularly with students of color and struggling students. This section will also help you improve your relations with students of color, strengthen your classroom management skills, and design culturally relevant standards-based lesson plans.

In the three chapters in **Part III, Getting Help From the "Village": How to Maximize Your Relations With Parents, Colleagues, and School Leaders,** you will learn how to work more effectively with parents (especially parents of color) and non-English-speaking parents. In addition to learning about the benefits of improving your relations with parents, you will learn actual scripts that you can use when you meet with parents. This section will also help you strengthen your relations with your colleagues (especially with colleagues of color) and help you get what you need from school leaders.

The conclusion contains a final story about a beginning teacher and a list of Confidence Boosters.

ABOUT THE BOOK'S TITLE

During his first campaign for president, Barack Obama often told the American public, "Yes, we can! Yes, we can!" On the night that he won the election, he began to chant, "Yes, we can! Yes, we can!" and audience members began to repeat this slogan. That night was momentous, for it marked the first time in U.S. history that a Black person had won the nation's highest office. It made a country that had a strong racist history look better. It made countless Americans, especially African Americans, feel better. It was a night of hope.

Regardless of how you feel about politics and regardless of your political affiliation, our goal in using *Yes, You Can!* as the title of this book is to provide you with practical strategies, advice, and hope—mainly hope about your ability to become a great educator of *all* students, especially students who have historically been underserved by the U.S. public school system such as African Americans, Latinos, and low-income students. As authors who have a nearly 60-year combined history as K–12 and university educators, we want to inspire you to keep teaching, even when the going gets tough. In addition to helping you to become more confident and persistent, we believe that this book will help the nation's youth by increasing their chances of having a confident, effective, and well-qualified teacher: you.

NOTES ABOUT THIS BOOK

- In the remainder of this book, we use the term *African American* to refer to all individuals who can be categorized by the racial designation of *Black*.
- All of the stories contained in this book are true. However, in several cases, we have changed the names of the main character or other individuals to protect their identities.
- In some cases, the TC Study results exceed 100 percent because percentages were rounded.

Part I

Do You *Really* Love *All of Them?*

Assessing Your Teaching Self-Confidence About Working With Various Types of Students

1 Fear, Income, Gender, and Other Issues

Why Your Teaching Self-Confidence Matters

MEET MICHAELA, A FRUSTRATED NEW TEACHER

In August 2012, Michaela was frustrated. The previous June—at the end of her first year of full-time teaching—she had received a "pink slip" notifying her that she would be laid off. Although the principal at the underperforming urban high school where she had worked had told her that she had done a great job, budget problems forced school district officials to lay off Michaela and all of the teachers who lacked seniority. For 24-year-old Michaela, the pink slip was the final slap in the face.

Michaela was disappointed and wondered if she'd have a job during the next school term. She was also angry. Her first full year of teaching had been extremely difficult. In one of her classes, two pregnant ninth graders almost had a fistfight one day. Furthermore, several of her students were arrested during the school year or were placed in her class after they were released from a local juvenile detention facility. No matter how hard she tried, some students refused to cooperate and defied her class rules. None of her teacher education training had prepared her for this! In fact, during the school year, Michaela often wondered whether or not she had chosen the right career. By the end of the year, she was even thinking that she would eventually change careers and abandon teaching completely.

But in August, Michaela received the great news that school district officials would rehire her. One official informed her that her former principal had requested that she be reassigned to the same high school. A few weeks later, the principal notified her that once again, she would be teaching freshman English. However, she would also be teaching eleventh-grade English for the first time. Although Michaela was happy to have her job back, she was terrified about teaching a higher grade level, especially when she only had a short time to prepare lesson plans and move into her classroom before the first day of school arrived.

EXERCISE   Now It's Your Turn

1. If you were Michaela, what would you do to make the beginning of the new school year as stress free as possible?

_____

_____

_____

_____

2. If you were one of Michaela's colleagues, what advice would you give her about teaching a new grade level for the first time?

_____

_____

_____

_____

CHAPTER HIGHLIGHTS

In the previous exercise, we asked you to put yourself in Michaela's shoes and to think of advice that you could give her, because as a teacher—especially if you are a beginning teacher—there will be times when you will feel just as Michaela did: uncertain about one or more aspects of your job. Also, after you gain more teaching experience, you might be asked to serve as a mentor to one or more beginning teachers or you may voluntarily choose to mentor new teachers at your school. Throughout this book, we will give you advice that can make your teaching career (especially your first years) less stressful. In this chapter, we will share some basic facts about teaching, describe the Teacher Confidence (TC) Study, ask you to complete several professional growth exercises, and explain why you need to examine your confidence levels about (a) your ability to treat all students fairly, (b) your ability to teach students from various income levels, and (c) your ability to teach males and females. We conclude the chapter with a summary and practical advice pertaining to the main topics of this chapter.

Six Basic Facts About Teaching

Before we describe the TC Study, here are some basic facts that you should keep in mind:

1. Yes, you made a wise decision.

In case you are wondering, as Michaela did, whether or not you made the right decision by becoming a teacher, we can assure you that you did. During the time that I (Gail) was a Peace Corps Volunteer in Africa, the Peace Corps' motto was "The Toughest Job You'll Ever Love." We believe that this motto also applies to teaching. Teaching is difficult for many of the reasons that we mentioned in the Introduction and others that we'll explain later. However, if you stick with it, you can definitely learn to love it, and you can have a very rewarding teaching career. In fact, it can become "the toughest job that you'll ever love."

2. No teacher is perfect.

If you strive to do your best and refuse to give up, you can become a good teacher and possibly even a great teacher. However, you will never become a perfect teacher, because no human being is perfect. In fact, when you read stories about mistakes that we made and that other educators have made, this will become even more apparent to you.

3. No teacher knows everything.

Good teachers realize that life is a learning experience, that they don't know everything, and that no matter how long they've been teaching or how much experience they have, they must be willing to learn new information, strategies, and so on.

4. Through hard work, you can become an outstanding teacher.

The strategies and professional growth exercises throughout this book will move you closer to the goal of becoming an outstanding teacher of all students, especially African American students and other students of color. So don't take shortcuts. We hope that you will complete every exercise and be as honest with yourself as possible.

5. Choosing to become a successful teacher of all students, especially African American students and other students of color, is a great confidence-building mindset to adopt.

A good foundation can be built upon many times. As a baseball player, I (Rufus) failed seven out of 10 times. Nevertheless, for a hitter in baseball, that is considered to be very, very, successful! It is all about how we view success. We pay millions of dollars per year to watch players fail seven out of 10 times! In education, we can't let this happen. My point to you is that from the very beginning of your teaching career until the end, success should be your goal. Striving for success will build your self-confidence. However, it is important not to have unrealistic expectations. Your bar should be very high for situations that you have control over: how you treat and view students, the quality of instruction that you provide to them, developing a fair and effective classroom management system, how you treat and view students' parents; and so on. Adopting the correct mindset is one of the main factors that will determine the degree of your success with all students, but especially with African American students and other students of color.

6. Fearfulness and a refusal to face your fears can prevent you from becoming a successful teacher, especially of African American students and other students of color.

Fear is such an important topic that in the next sections, we elaborate on it and give you opportunities to examine any fears or uncertainties that you have about your teaching ability.

E X E R C I S E   Exploring Your Fears and Concerns About Teaching

1. What aspects of being a teacher do you fear or are you most uncertain about and why?

_____

_____

_____

_____

2. Whom, if anyone (parents, specific types of students, other teachers, specific types of staff, school leaders, etc.), do you fear and why?

_____

_____

_____

_____

(Continued)

(Continued)

3. Where did these fears come from?

_____

_____

_____

_____

4. Now, examine your answers to the previous questions and explain what you can learn from them.

_____

_____

_____

_____

THE LINK BETWEEN FEAR AND SELF-CONFIDENCE

Michaela, the beginning teacher whom we described earlier, lacked confidence about her ability to teach eleventh graders for two main reasons: She had never taught this grade level before, and she also admitted to us that eleventh graders tend to be physically bigger than ninth graders. But underneath these concerns lurked fear. Fear and a lack of confidence are closely related. In Michaela's case, as a teacher in her twenties, she feared that older students might not treat a young teacher respectfully. More importantly, she feared that she would not be successful in working with this grade level of students. As in Michaela's case, often when teachers lack confidence about their ability to effectively perform a job-related task, the real issue is that they are fearful. Fear can lead to a lack of self-confidence and a lack of self-efficacy. It can also result in defensiveness, unfair treatment, and other problems. In order to work effectively with all students (especially African American students and other students of color), you must treat all students fairly.

Wanting to be treated fairly is a basic human desire, and K–12 students are no different. However, various students, such as African Americans, Latinos, and Native Americans—groups that have historically been subjected to racism, oppression, and unfair treatment in the United States—may be more likely than other students to view teacher attitudes and behaviors as unfair, even if teachers may not realize this.[1] As a teacher, you may assume that you are treating all students fairly, but students may infer the opposite. By making a conscious decision to treat all students fairly, you can avoid a lot of problems, especially in terms of discipline problems, which we'll talk about extensively in Part II. Therefore, in addition to knowing *what* you fear about teaching, you also need to know *where* you lack confidence. The next exercise (which focuses on *fairness*) and other exercises throughout this book will help you identify specific problems that can decrease your effectiveness as a teacher.

E X E R C I S E   Measuring Your Teaching Self-Confidence About Treating All Students Fairly

Please respond to the following question with V = *Very Confident*, S = *Somewhat Confident*, or N = *Not Confident at All*.

1. How confident are you about your ability to treat all students fairly? _____

2. Now examine your answer to the previous question and explain what you can learn from it.

_____

_____

_____

_____

THE TEACHER CONFIDENCE STUDY

If your answer to the previous question revealed that you are *not confident* or only *somewhat confident* about your ability to treat all students fairly, you can sigh with relief. You are human, and lots of other teachers—even many who have a lot more teaching experience than you do—feel the same way. In an effort to learn more about teachers' self-confidence in their ability to be fair and other topics, I (Gail) created the Teacher Confidence (TC) Study. The study was based on a questionnaire that I distributed to 293 *preservice* (interns who were finishing their course work in a teacher education program) and *more experienced* teachers who attended professional development workshops that I conducted in California. Like most K–12 teachers nationwide, the majority of the respondents were White females. The TC Study participants answered numerous questions and then were asked to examine their responses and explain what they learned from them. (You can learn more about the questionnaire and the respondents in the Appendix section.)

Throughout this book, you'll be reading a lot about the TC Study, and you'll also have numerous opportunities to assess your teaching self-confidence—especially about working with African American students and other students of color, struggling students, and parents—and to compare and contrast your answers with those of the TC Study respondents. In fact, in the previous exercise, you already answered one of the questions, so now it's time to compare and contrast your responses with theirs.

Figure 1.1   What the TC Study Respondents Said About Treating All Students Fairly

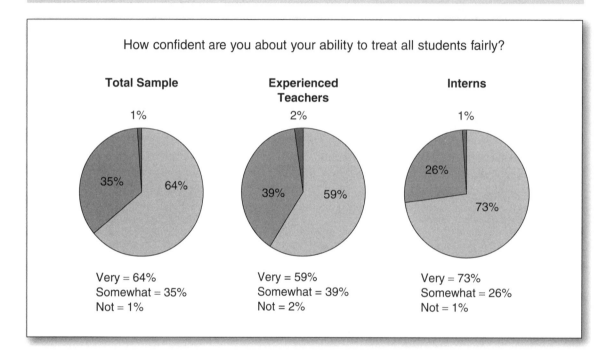

How confident are you about your ability to treat all students fairly?

Total Sample

1%

35%   64%

Very = 64%
Somewhat = 35%
Not = 1%

Experienced Teachers

2%

39%   59%

Very = 59%
Somewhat = 39%
Not = 2%

Interns

1%

26%

73%

Very = 73%
Somewhat = 26%
Not = 1%

Like you, the TC Study respondents were asked to measure their level of confidence about fairness (see Figure 1.1). Surprisingly, a higher percentage of interns than more experienced teachers said that they were very confident about their ability to treat all students fairly. One likely reason is that because they had more teaching experience, the experienced teachers were more aware of how difficult it is to do this.

Comments that the interns wrote illustrate that this might have indeed been the case. For example, a Hispanic female with no teaching experience wrote, "I'm very confident I can and will be a great teacher regardless of the students' race, socio-economic background, or if their parents are supportive or not." An African American female who had no teaching experience wrote:

I am a very confident individual in dealing with human beings of every race or creed. I love diversity and I embrace every culture. I am compassionate and know how to deal with human behavior. I work in retail, so you figure out what to say, and how, in giving people what they need. I come from a very diverse background and growing up poverty-stricken, I assimilated to the mainstream environment.

Other interns wrote more realistic comments. For instance, a Latina with no teaching experience said, "I have no real teaching experience and don't really know what to expect." An African American female with one year of teaching experience said, "I've learned that I need to build my confidence in connecting with all students." An Asian American male who had no teaching experience wrote:

> For the most part, having no teaching experience, I can really only speculate about my future performance. I'm very confident that I can instill equality and help any student regardless of background, but having never done it, I can't be fully confident.

At the end of this chapter, we will share some advice about how you can treat all students fairly, and in Part II, we'll return to this topic and examine carefully why it's so important for you to do your best to treat all students, especially African American students and other students of color, fairly. But for now, please reflect on what you learned from the TC Study respondents.

EXERCISE   What You Learned From the TC Study Respondents

1. What are the most important points that you learned from the TC Study respondents' answers?

_____

_____

_____

_____

2. Which comments differ from your views and why?

_____

_____

_____

_____

(Continued)

(Continued)

3. Which comments are most similar to your views and why?

_____

_____

_____

_____

FAIRNESS AND INCOME

The ability to treat all students fairly is linked to many issues, including the way students look, their race, stereotypes, teachers' beliefs, teachers' upbringing, and students' backgrounds.[2] For example, researchers have found that teachers tend to have lower expectations of low-income students and higher expectations for middle-class and upper-class students. In terms of discipline, teachers are also more likely to penalize students of color and low-income students than other students,[3] and upper-class African American students experience many of the same negative schooling experiences as low-income African Americans.[4] Consequently, the ability to work effectively with all students, but especially with students of color, requires you to examine your beliefs and measure your teaching self-confidence about *many* issues, including seemingly unrelated ones such as income and gender. Therefore, in the following sections, we'd like for you to examine your teaching self-confidence related to students' income and gender, learn what the TC Study respondents said, and compare and contrast your answers to theirs.

Effectively Teaching Low-Income Students

Because of the recent worldwide economic downturn, the number of children in poverty has increased. In the United States in 2009, for example, more than 15 million children under age 18 lived in poverty.[5] Each year, over one million children in the United States "experience homelessness," and approximately 200,000 are homeless each day.[6] These statistics suggest that at some point in your teaching career, it's very likely that you'll work with low-income students, especially since teacher turnover rates tend to be greater in low-income schools. This means that low-income schools are more apt to have teaching vacancies than other schools. If you're hired to work in an impoverished community, working with low-income students will become a daily reality for you. Furthermore, African American, Latino, and Native American students tend to be overrepresented among the students who live in poverty. Because one of our primary objectives is to equip you with information that will help you work successfully with all students, especially with African American students and other students of color, measuring your teaching confidence about your ability to work effectively with low-income students is important.

EXERCISE   Effectively Teaching Low-Income Students

1. How confident are you about your ability to effectively teach low-income students and why?

_____

_____

_____

_____

2. What can you learn from your answer to the previous question?

_____

_____

_____

_____

Figure 1.2   What the TC Study Respondents Said About Working With Low-Income Students

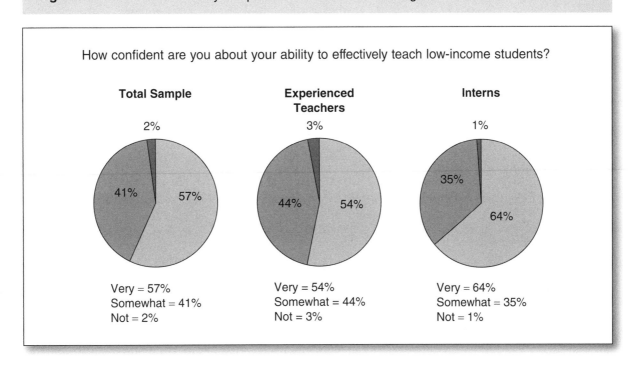

How confident are you about your ability to effectively teach low-income students?

Total Sample

2%
41%   57%

Very = 57%
Somewhat = 41%
Not = 2%

Experienced Teachers

3%
44%   54%

Very = 54%
Somewhat = 44%
Not = 3%

Interns

1%
35%
64%

Very = 64%
Somewhat = 35%
Not = 1%

In explaining his views about working with low-income students, an Asian American male high school math teacher with 4–5 years of teaching experience admitted, "I have biases toward low-income students." An African American female intern with no teaching experience wrote, "I am skeptical about what I will experience at a low-income school." A Latina intern with one year of teaching experience said, "I don't feel completely confident working in low-income schools."

Whereas many of the respondents expressed concern about their ability to work with low-income students, others felt differently. For example, a White female who had taught high school for 2–3 years said, "I have always thrived on working with lower-income students who really need my help and guidance." An African American high school social studies teacher who had taught for 27 years wrote,

> As a result of my race, I had the choice to teach in a high-income school, because the school needed racial balance. But my priority has always been low-income students because the need was always there. This is how I would like to end my teaching career: helping and providing assistance to low-income African American and Latino students.

Now, please take some time to reflect on what you learned from Figure 1.2 and the TC Study respondents' comments.

EXERCISE   What You Learned From the TC Study Respondents

1. What are the most important points that you learned from the TC Study respondents' answers?

_____

_____

_____

_____

2. Which comments differ from your views and why?

_____

_____

_____

_____

3. Which comments are most similar to your views and why?

_____

_____

_____

_____

Working Effectively With Middle-Class Students

In addition to understanding your confidence level about teaching low-income students, you also need to examine your views about other income groups. Although African American and Latino students are overrepresented among the students who live in poverty, substantial numbers of them also come from middle-class and even upper-class backgrounds. In fact, since the 1960s, the African American middle-class has grown tremendously. Although most teachers come from middle-class backgrounds, many teachers lump all students of color together and fail to realize that there is a lot of income diversity within each racial or ethnic group. This failure causes teachers to assume that all African American and Latino students come from low-income backgrounds, and often, middle-class students and their parents are treated accordingly. For example, in _Black Students. Middle Class Teachers_, Dr. Jawanza Kunjufu wrote that because of stereotypes and teaching inadequacies, teachers from middle-class backgrounds often fail dismally with African American students.[7] The next exercise encourages you to examine your confidence level about teaching middle-class students.

EXERCISE   Effectively Teaching Middle-Class Students

1. How confident are you about your ability to effectively teach middle-class students and why?

_____

_____

_____

_____

(Continued)

(Continued)

2. What can you learn from your answer to the previous question?

_____

_____

_____

_____

Figure 1.3 What the TC Study Respondents Said About Working With Middle-Class Students

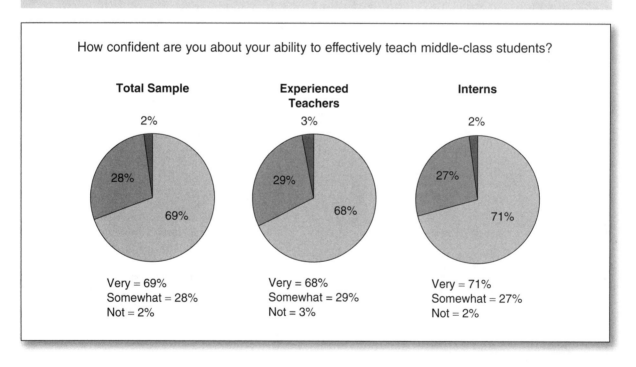

How confident are you about your ability to effectively teach middle-class students?

Total Sample

2%

28%

69%

Very = 69%
Somewhat = 28%
Not = 2%

Experienced Teachers

3%

29%

68%

Very = 68%
Somewhat = 29%
Not = 3%

Interns

2%

27%

71%

Very = 71%
Somewhat = 27%
Not = 2%

A White female high school teacher with more than five years of teaching experience wrote, "I question my efficacy as a teacher for students other than the middle- to upper-class student." Conversely, a White male high school teacher who had taught for more than 20 years stated, "I have grown in confidence as a teacher, teaching in an urban setting. My experience is in low-income Latino/African American school settings. I am more comfortable in this setting than I would be in a middle-class [W]hite classroom." Now, please take some time to reflect on what you learned from Figure 1.3 and the comments in this section.

EXERCISE   What You Learned From the TC Study Respondents

1. What are the most important points that you learned from the TC Study respondents' answers?

_____

_____

_____

_____

2. Which comments differ from your views and why?

_____

_____

_____

_____

3. Which comments are most similar to your views and why?

_____

_____

_____

_____

_____

Working Effectively With Upper-Class Students

Most U.S. cities and most public school districts have three categories of schools: low-income, middle-class, and upper-class. Schools in wealthier areas tend to be associated with higher standardized test scores, more overt parental involvement, stronger political influence, and better resources. They also tend to have fewer students of color.[8]

In spite of this, if you end up teaching at a school that only has a small number of students of color in it, it's important for you to be aware of your attitudes, beliefs, and treatment of these students. Otherwise, you could end up viewing and treating these students in harmful ways. Similarly, if you have unexamined fears, stereotypes, and prejudices associated with upper-class individuals, you may unknowingly engage in biased behaviors toward White and nonwhite students who come from upper-class backgrounds. Understanding your underlying beliefs and confidence level about teaching these students can prevent you from falling into this trap. The next exercise allows you to explore your confidence level in this regard.

E X E R C I S E Effectively Teaching Upper-Class Students

1. How confident are you about your ability to effectively teach upper-class students and why?

_____

_____

_____

_____

2. What can you learn from your answer to the previous question?

_____

_____

_____

_____

Figure 1.4 What the TC Study Respondents Said About Working With High-Income Students

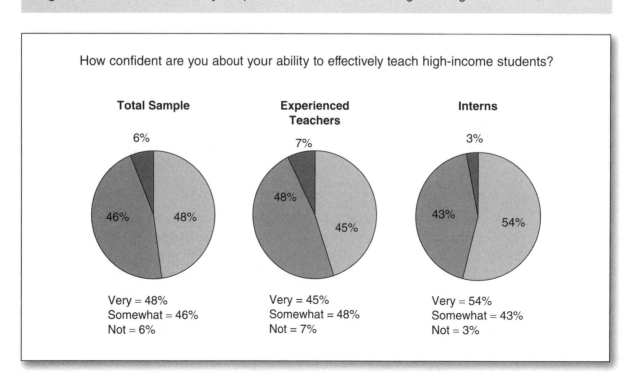

How confident are you about your ability to effectively teach high-income students?

Total Sample

6%

46% 48%

Very = 48%
Somewhat = 46%
Not = 6%

Experienced Teachers

7%

48%

45%

Very = 45%
Somewhat = 48%
Not = 7%

Interns

3%

43% 54%

Very = 54%
Somewhat = 43%
Not = 3%

In explaining her feelings about working with high-income students, an African American high school music teacher with more than five years of teaching experience wrote, "Higher income people, kids, and families intimidate me." A White female middle school teacher who had taught for more than five years wrote, "I am confident working at a public school with suburban low-income kids. In the high-income areas, I can do the same good job of teaching, but the parents in those high-income areas will be a pain." Now, we'd like for you to reflect on what you learned from Figure 1.4 and the TC Study respondents' comments in this section.

E X E R C I S E   What You Learned From the TC Study Respondents

1. What are the most important points that you learned from the TC Study respondents' answers?

_____

_____

_____

_____

2. Which comments differ from your views and why?

_____

_____

_____

_____

3. Which comments are most similar to your views and why?

_____

_____

_____

_____

GENDER AND CONFIDENCE

In spite of the progress that has been made in the United States so that both males and females can have equal rights, gender biases and sexism are still prevalent in the workplace and even in schools. Many people still harbor stereotypes about males and also about females. Some believe, for example, that males can do better in certain subjects, such as mathematics and science, than females.

Research has shown that males and females tend to have different K–12 schooling experiences. Negative labels are more likely to be placed on males; males are more likely to be labeled as *hyperactive*; males are more likely to be placed in special education classes; males are more likely to be labeled as *behavior problems*; and males are more likely to be suspended and expelled from school.

Although White males, especially those from low-income backgrounds, often have negative schooling experiences, African American and Latino males are extremely more likely to do so.[9] One of the main reasons is that female teachers in particular—who dominate the K–12 teaching force—have not examined or addressed their fears and mental baggage about male students, especially about African American and Latino males.[10]

Therefore, knowing how you feel about your ability to work effectively with males and females is important so that you don't subconsciously give students the impression that you believe that they are incapable of excelling in your class simply because of their gender. This is why the TC Study questionnaire contained questions about gender. In Chapter 2, we elaborate on the schooling experiences of males of color, especially Latino and African American males. Now, however, we'd like for you to complete the following exercise.

EXERCISE   **Teaching Boys and Girls**

1. How confident are you about your ability to effectively teach girls and why?

_____

_____

_____

_____

2. How confident are you about your ability to effectively teach boys and why?

_____

_____

_____

_____

3. Now, examine your answers and explain what you can learn from them.

_____

_____

_____

_____

Figure 1.5 What the TC Study Respondents Said About Teaching Boys and Girls

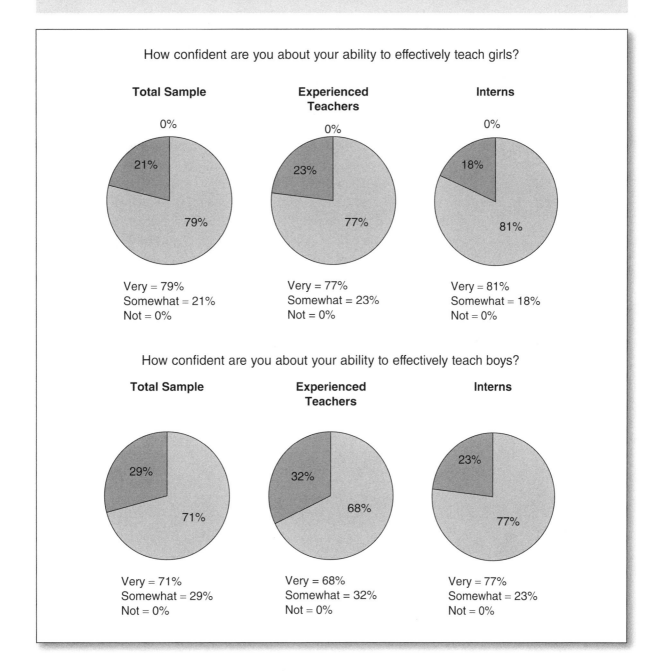

Effectively Teaching Females

A female elementary school teacher who had taught for more than five years clearly didn't understand why teachers need to examine their beliefs about males and females, for she wrote, "Gender is not an achievement issue." However, a female high school teacher who had taught for 4–5 years indicated that even students themselves can be sexist in how they view teachers. She stated, "I feel students listen more to a male better than a female. Therefore, my skills can always be improved." A male high school mathematics teacher who had only taught for a year admitted, "I am somewhat insecure with girls because I have too much respect for females." A female intern with no teaching experience shared a similar concern: "I am fearful of problems in class because of my gender." In Chapter 2, we return to the topic of females when we explain what the respondents said about African American female students.

Effectively Teaching Males

A female who had taught high school English for more than five years wrote, "I am more confident with girls than boys." However, several of the respondents who said that they were very confident about all aspects of their teaching ability wrote comments questioning their abilities. "I am probably more confident than I am able. Maybe, too confident," a male high school science teacher with more than five years of teaching experience stated. Another male high school teacher who had taught for more than 20 years said, "I never found the kid I couldn't teach."

As we previously stated, in Chapter 2, we spend more time focusing on gender because many respondents wrote comments that were specifically about African American males or African American females. Now, please reflect on what you learned from Figure 1.5 and the TC Study respondents' comments in this section.

E X E R C I S E   What You Learned From the TC Study Respondents

1. What are the most important points that you learned from the TC Study respondents' replies?

_____

_____

_____

_____

2. Which comments differ from your views and why?

_____

_____

_____

_____

3. Which comments are most similar to your views and why?

_____

_____

_____

_____

CONCLUSION

What We Can Learn From the TC Study

At the beginning of this chapter, we introduced you to Michaela, a second-year teacher who was fearful about teaching a new grade level. We explained that fear and a lack of confidence are linked and that a lack of confidence about many issues can prevent you from becoming an effective teacher, especially with students of color. Throughout the chapter, we asked you to examine your confidence levels about your ability to treat all students fairly and to teach low-income, middle-class, and upper-class students (both male and female), because sometimes, teachers aren't aware that they harbor income and gender biases against students.

- The TC Study respondents were less likely to be very confident about their ability to effectively teach upper-class students than middle-class or low-income students.
- The TC Study respondents were more likely to be very confident about their ability to effectively teach middle-class students than low-income students.
- The TC Study respondents were more likely to be very confident about their ability to effectively teach girls than boys.
- More than one-third of the TC Study respondents admitted that they were not very confident about their ability to treat all students fairly.
- The interns were more likely than the experienced teachers to rate themselves as very confident in all areas.
- Many White teachers and many teachers of color expressed a lack of confidence about the topics.

We conclude this chapter with advice, strategies, professional growth exercises, and recommended readings that can help you increase your confidence levels about working with all students, regardless of their income level or gender.

ADVICE AND STRATEGIES

1. Don't fool yourself.

One of the main reasons why some teachers fail dismally with African American students and other students of color is that they are in denial and claim to be colorblind to racial differences, income differences, gender differences, cultural differences, and so on. Therefore, it pays to be honest with yourself about your beliefs and biases and to seek to remedy them.

2. Look beneath the surface.

Explore all of your responses to the exercises in this chapter in detail and look for the hidden messages. For example, if, like the TC Study respondents, you learned that you feel less confident about your ability to effectively teach upper-class students than middle-class or low-income students, identify the real reason. It is likely that one of the reasons why many respondents felt this way is that they are fearful about working in an environment that is more likely to be associated with high expectations and rigor. Additionally, if you found that you felt more confident about your ability to work with middle-class students than low-income students, try to determine whether the underlying reason is that you associated low-income with African American and Latino students and middle-class with White students. Consequently, a hidden fear of working with African American and Latino students might be the true culprit that you need to face and address.

3. Be confident, but not overly confident.

Obviously, one of our main goals for writing this book is to help you become more confident about your ability to work effectively with all students, especially students of color. Confidence is needed, but so is realism. When people become cocky and overconfident, they are likely to fall flat on their face and fail. That's why it's so important for you to be honest as you examine your fears and assess your level of confidence about each topic. The fact that the interns were more likely than the experienced teachers to say that they were very confident about working with low-income, middle-class, and upper-class students and about working with boys and girls makes us suspect that they were in for a rude awakening during their first year of teaching.

4. Remember that treating students fairly is not the same as treating all students equally.

There's no way that you'll be able to treat all students equally and have positive results. Students arrive at school with different experiences and needs, which can impact how they interact with you. One way to ensure that you are treating students fairly is to keep a paraphrased version of a famous biblical commandment in mind: "Treat others in the manner in which you would like to be treated." In other words, when you deal with students, try to put yourself in their shoes whenever possible.

Also, always keep in mind that you are the person in authority. That puts you in a very powerful position. If you are having a bad day or you have been asked the same question several times and are fed up, don't take it out on the next student who asks the question or the next student with whom you have to deal. Take a step back and try to put yourself in the student's place.

Additionally, we advise you to keep assessing your behavior. For instance, simply asking yourself, "Do I say nice things to certain students and not to others?" can help you become aware of negative differential treatment. This strategy was one that helped us personally during our K–12 teaching years. For example, when I (Rufus) was a new social studies middle school teacher, I made the mistake of not complimenting my African American students enough. The underlying motive was that as an African American teacher, I didn't want the nonblack students to accuse me of giving the Black students preferential treatment. My unfair treatment toward the African American students became clear to me one day during a cooperative learning activity.

All of the African American students in a particular class were sitting together. I informed them that their choice to work together as a group wasn't acceptable, and I wanted them to mix in with the rest of the class. In essence, I told the African American students that they couldn't sit with each other. In a respectful manner, the students questioned my decision. When I explained my rationale, they looked at each other and then at me and replied almost in unison, "The White students are sitting together!" They were absolutely correct. Not only did they teach me an important lesson, but I backed down and allowed them to continue to work together as a group. This experience taught me the hard way that as educators, we often expect students to accept our decisions that are rooted in insecurity and fear.

During that same school year, the African American students worked together on some amazing projects. They were top-notch, and perhaps the outcome would have been different if I had destroyed their group. Surprisingly, the White students never complained to me about the "Black group." In fact, all of the groups worked well together. In retrospect, I believe that I was able to avoid a potential huge racial conflict because of the respect and the relationship that I had developed with students by treating them fairly in other situations.

5. Keep working on each problem or issue that surfaces.

As you are reading this book, and long after you finish it, we want you to keep growing. Engaging in ongoing self-reflection, learning from mistakes, and identifying and working on concerns will help you to continue to grow personally and professionally.

6. If you are assigned to teach a new course at the last minute, try the following strategies:

- Affirm yourself. You must believe in yourself; if you don't, you will not succeed. Once that has taken place, get busy with preparation. Be prepared to work late into the night until you are ready to meet your students on the first day.
- As soon as you can get a list of the students' names, ask a school secretary where you can locate their cumulative files. Read the files in order to learn what you can about your students, but don't prejudge them. Just because a student may have had problems with a previous teacher does not necessarily mean that the student will have problems with you.
- Develop lessons that are short and interactive. Don't spend too much time lecturing. There are many lesson plans available online and from your county and state agencies and also organizations that use grade-level standards as a foundation. Find them and use them.
- Ask veteran teachers for help and sample lesson plans, especially those who have taught the subject and grade level that you have been assigned to teach.

- Finally, if you are assigned to teach a new course at the last minute, don't take it personally. During my (Rufus's) first seven years of teaching, I had no idea what I was going to be teaching until the week before school started. In my case, however, I actually requested the difficult students. I also asked for the larger classes. Since I was a physical education teacher and former athlete, I was used to teaching classes with 55 students in them. In physical education classes, the students had to move around, and they were from diverse backgrounds. Many were from rival gangs, and some were physically disabled. Therefore, whenever an administrator informed me that I was going to have to teach a class of 35 students in a traditional classroom setting, I thought, "Are you kidding me?" In comparison to teaching the large physical education classes, this setup sounded great to me. The bottom line is that over time, your teaching confidence will grow, and you will be less likely to panic if you are assigned to teach a new course at the last minute.

Professional Growth Strategy: Create a Personalized *Yes, I Can!* Journal

As soon as possible, create a journal in which to record your thoughts; lessons learned; confidence-building tips; teaching strategies; classroom management strategies; strategies to improve your relations with parents, colleagues, and administrators; and additional information that you will learn from this book. Refer to and update your *Yes, I Can!* journal on an ongoing basis. The following questions can help you apply what you learned from this chapter to your journal.

APPLYING WHAT YOU LEARNED TO YOUR *YES, I CAN!* JOURNAL

1. What was your income level growing up?
2. How did your income level influence your beliefs about individuals from other income groups?
3. How did your income level influence your beliefs about African Americans, Latinos, Native Americans, Asian Americans, and Whites?
4. After reading this chapter, what issues related to treating students fairly; working with low-income, middle-class, and upper-class students; and working with boys and girls do you still need to address?
5. What remaining questions do you have about the topics that were covered in this chapter?

Teaching in a Racially Diverse World 2

Examining Your Teaching Self-Confidence About Working With Students of Color *and* White Students

A few days before the 2012 U.S. election that would determine which candidate, Governor Mitt Romney or the incumbent, President Barack Obama, would become the nation's next president, we were reminded of the main message that we want you to learn from this chapter: When people are in need, race, income level, gender, age, and other differences don't really matter. This message definitely applies to students, because all students *need* help from good teachers. However, because historically many public school educators have underserved students of color, these students desperately need good teachers. Consequently, they need for you to strive to become the best teacher that you can become. The following two stories emphasize this message about need.

"WHEN PEOPLE ARE IN NEED": TWO STORIES WITH THE SAME MESSAGE

A State Senator and Medical Doctor's Story

One day, shortly before the 2012 election for U.S. president, while listening to a local radio program, we heard North Carolina Senator Eric Mansfield share a story about need. According to Senator Mansfield, who is also a medical doctor, several years earlier, he had been in Louisiana to aid victims of a natural disaster. Many people needed medical attention. However, one injured White resident made it clear that he was a racist, and no matter how sick he was, he did not want help from any "Black person," even if the individual happened to be a trained physician.

A nurse tried to convince the man that Dr. Mansfield was highly qualified to treat him. Furthermore, she informed him that at that moment, Dr. Mansfield was the only physician who was available to provide the medical care that he needed. Nevertheless, the man continued to refuse Dr. Mansfield's help. Finally, in a moment of desperation, the man's wife intervened. She told her husband, "Look: You need to get over your issues and let this doctor help you!" And that's what it took. One woman's courage and candor not only caused her husband to put his antiblack prejudice aside (even if only temporarily) and allow Dr. Mansfield to treat him, but probably also saved his life.

A Civil Rights Attorney's Story

As we began to discuss Dr. Mansfield's story with each other, we remembered a similar story that we'd heard years earlier. At the time, we were attending an event at a California university featuring a prominent civil rights attorney. During the evening, the attorney shared many stories about her work as an advocate for marginalized, mistreated, and low-income individuals. All of the stories were fascinating, including the one about the time when she was literally thrown out of a Los Angeles building. However, as with Dr. Mansfield's story, the most riveting story underscored a message about need.

According to the attorney, early in her career, she had worked as a public defender in a southern state. One of the defendants whom she was assigned to represent was an outspoken White racist. This man had a violent history, was a repeat offender, and had recently been arrested for committing a heinous crime. As a result, he was eligible for the death penalty.

When the petite attorney first visited him in jail and introduced herself to him, the man was outraged. He was offended that an African American woman would represent him in court. He boldly called her the "N word" and informed her that neither she nor any other Black person would represent him in court.

Although the attorney had several options at this time—and, like Dr. Mansfield, could've washed her hands of the matter—instead, she resorted to candor and courage. She told the prisoner, "I am the only person who is standing between you and the death penalty. You decide what you want to do." Just as the sick Louisiana racist's wife helped her husband realize how much he needed Dr. Mansfield's help, the attorney's words changed the inmate's attitude. He had come from a low-income background, yet this White man had always believed that he was superior to African Americans, even educated ones. But now he realized that because he was in a hopeless situation, he needed an advocate—even if she happened to be an African American—to fight for his life.

From that point on, the inmate began to cooperate with the attorney. Over time, she learned that during childhood, he had experienced horrific abuse. This abuse contributed to his life of crime. Although the attorney believed that he needed to be held accountable for his crimes and would always be a danger to society, she also believed that the man had never been taught the values and morals that a child who had grown up under normal conditions would've learned. In the end, she was able to convince a judge that despite the fact that the man was indeed guilty of the crimes of which he was accused, his life should be spared for humanitarian reasons. The judge agreed and sentenced him to life in prison instead of execution.

EXERCISE   Now, It's Your Turn

Both of the aforementioned stories contain messages about race relations, candor, courage, and need.

1. Which story resonated with you the most or had the strongest impact on you and why?

_____

_____

_____

_____

2. Can you be candid with yourself regarding how you really feel about race relations and racial issues? Why or why not?

_____

_____

_____

_____

3. Can you be candid with your family members, friends, and acquaintances about race relations and racial issues? Why or why not?

_____

_____

_____

_____

CHAPTER HIGHLIGHTS

In this chapter, we delve more deeply into race relations, specifically about the importance of striving to work effectively with students of color *and* White students. We also share the related Teacher Confidence (TC) Study results and ask you to examine your confidence levels about working with students of color and White students, and to compare and contrast your self-ratings with the TC Study respondents'. In each section, we emphasize the message that when people are in need, racial differences don't really matter. We conclude the chapter with pertinent advice and strategies.

EXERCISE **Teaching White Students Exercise**

1. How confident are you about your ability to effectively teach White male students and why?

_____

_____

_____

_____

2. How confident are you about your ability to effectively teach White female students and why?

_____

_____

_____

_____

3. Now, examine your answers and explain what you can learn from them.

_____

_____

_____

_____

WHY YOUR BELIEFS ABOUT TEACHING WHITE STUDENTS MATTER

Remember that one of our main goals for writing this book is to help you become more confident about your ability to work effectively with African

American students and other students of color by offering research, advice, and strategies. However, we have also emphasized that we want you to learn to work effectively with *all* students. This, of course, includes White students.

Since 1990, the number and percentages of White prekindergarten–12 students enrolled in public schools have decreased. In 1990, for example, 29 million (67 percent) White students were enrolled in comparison to 27.7 million (54 percent) in 2010.[1] In 2010, White students were more likely to be enrolled in public schools in the Midwest (70 percent) and Northeast (59 percent) than in the South (50 percent) and West (43 percent).[2] Most (62 percent) White students attend predominantly White schools. However, Whites who attend city schools (rather than schools in towns, suburbs, or rural areas) are more likely to attend schools that have higher concentrations of students of color.[3]

In spite of the smaller percentages of Whites in public schools than in previous eras, White students are still more likely than students of color, especially African Americans, Native Americans, and Latino students, to have positive schooling experiences. For example, Whites are more likely to have higher standardized test scores, graduate from high school, be prepared for college, and attend college. They are also less likely to drop out of school and are less likely to be suspended or expelled from school. Moreover, even when Whites attend schools with high concentrations of students of color, they are more likely to have positive school-related experiences. In one study that I (Gail) conducted, for example, Whites who attended a California high school that had a higher number of students of color than Whites were more likely than African American or Latino students to agree that most of their teachers were good teachers, that teachers treated them fairly, that most of their teachers were willing to give them extra help during class time, and that they had never experienced racism from teachers.[4]

However, results from that same California study revealed that some of the White students had a less-than-ideal experience. Several of the White females, for instance, said that they were fearful of African American male students whom they felt were harassing them, and the females stated that they felt unsafe at school. Second, the White males were more likely than the White females to report that they were having negative schooling experiences. Furthermore, Whites were almost equally as likely as African Americans to say that most of the information that they were learning in class and most of the homework assigned was not useful. They were also more likely than African American and Latino students to indicate that they had experienced racism from other students and more likely than African Americans and Latinos to say they had been sent to the office for misbehavior.[5]

The results from the California study clearly reveal that teachers must be careful not to make assumptions about White students. Also, the study suggests that the schooling experiences of some White students, especially those who attend schools in which they constitute less than the majority, could be better. As a teacher, regardless of what type of school at which you teach and how many White students are enrolled in your classes, the bottom line is that White students deserve a great education. Moreover, in spite of their decreased numbers in public K–12 schools, they still account for the majority of public school students. Therefore, their sheer numbers indicate that they matter and that their schooling needs cannot and should not be ignored. This is something that all teachers—White teachers and teachers of color—must remember. Now let's examine what the TC Study respondents said about their ability to effectively teach White students (see Figure 2.1).

Figure 2.1 What the TC Study Respondents Said About Effectively Teaching White Students

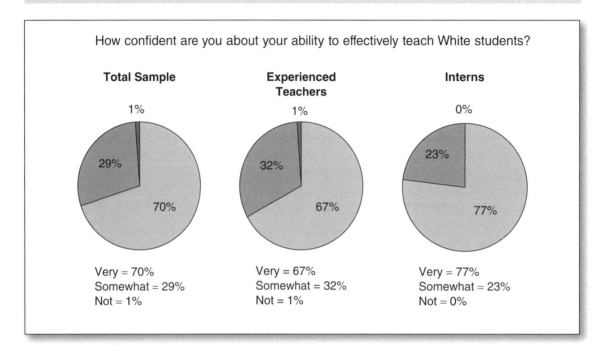

How confident are you about your ability to effectively teach White students?

Total Sample

1%
29%
70%

Very = 70%
Somewhat = 29%
Not = 1%

Experienced Teachers

1%
32%
67%

Very = 67%
Somewhat = 32%
Not = 1%

Interns

0%
23%
77%

Very = 77%
Somewhat = 23%
Not = 0%

Through their written comments, numerous TC Study respondents admitted that they felt more confident about their ability to work with students from racial backgrounds that were similar to their own than they were about working with other students. For example, a White male high school social studies teacher with more than five years of teaching experience stated that he worked "better with students with backgrounds similar to [his own]." An Asian American male middle school science teacher who had taught for more than five years made a similar comment: "I'm confident with what I've had experience with. I'm not sure about how confident I am with dealing with other races that I'm not familiar with." Conversely, a White female middle school language arts teacher with more than five years' teaching experience said:

> Ironically, I feel least confident teaching and working with students whose background is most like the background from which I came. It's not as motivating, and I don't really like where I came from. I also like the challenge of cultural difference because I am constantly learning.

An African American female elementary school teacher with more than five years of teaching experience said, "I have learned that because of my experience with the upper-class [W]hite and Asian populations that I'm not as confident in working with that demographic. I am confident with my teaching skills, but not in their acceptance of me." Another African American educator with more than five years of teaching experience admitted,

> Through my experience as an educator, I am more concerned about my ability to impact [W]hite children and families because of the racism I have encountered over the years. I find that I have to jump through hoops and over mountains to get the same respect of the [W]hite families compared to other races. I believe this is because they do not see me as an educator before they see me as [B]lack.

Now, we'd like for you to summarize what you learned from Figure 2.1 and the information that you just read.

EXERCISE   What You Learned From the TC Study Respondents

1. What are the most important points that you learned from the TC Study respondents' answers?

_____

_____

_____

_____

2. Which comments differ from your views and why?

_____

_____

_____

_____

3. Which comments are most similar to your views and why?

_____

_____

_____

_____

TEACHING AFRICAN AMERICAN AND OTHER STUDENTS OF COLOR

The schooling needs of White students are important, and White students still make up a large percentage of the K–12 public school population. However, in recent decades, as the number and percentages of White students in public schools have declined, the opposite is true for students of color. The paradox is that while public schools have become more racially diverse, the teaching force has remained predominantly White and mostly female. That means that during their K–12 schooling years, most students of color will primarily have teachers who come from a racial background that is vastly different from their own. As a teacher, it also means that you'll more than likely be teaching students who come from backgrounds that may be very different from your own. This is why it's crucial for you to do your best to learn how to work effectively with all students, but especially with students of color.

Because they constitute the three largest groups of students of color, the following sections only focus on three groups of students of color: Asian Americans, Latinos, and African Americans. In 2010, for example,

> Native Hawaiian/Pacific Islander and American Indian/Alaska Native students each represented 1 percent or less of student enrollment in all regions of the United States. . . . Students of two or more races made up 4 percent of enrollment in the West, 3 percent in the Midwest, and 2 percent each in the Northeast and South.[6]

However, although the next sections pertain to three groups of students of color, please keep in mind that there are many nonwhite racial and ethnic groups in U.S. public schools, and every single student, regardless of his or her race or ethnicity, deserves to receive an outstanding education. Now, we'd like for you to complete another exercise.

EXERCISE **Effectively Teaching Asian American Students**

1. How confident are you about your ability to effectively teach Asian American male students and why?

_____

_____

_____

_____

2. How confident are you about your ability to effectively teach Asian American females and why?

_____

_____

_____

_____

3. Now, examine your answers and explain what you can learn from them.

_____

_____

_____

_____

WHY YOUR BELIEFS ABOUT TEACHING ASIAN AMERICAN STUDENTS MATTER

Of the four main racial groups in the United States—Whites, Blacks, Latinos, and Asian Americans—Asian Americans constitute the smallest group. In 2010, for example, Asian Americans accounted for 4 percent of prekindergarten–12 public school students.[7] Although they have been referred to as the "model minority," Asian American students come from diverse backgrounds, and many have been underserved by the public school system. According to Dr. Derald Wing Sue, an expert on racism and racial diversity, "The term _Asian American_ technically encompasses some twenty-nine to thirty-two distinct identifiable Asian subgroups with their own culture, language, customs, and traditions. . . ."[8] Most Asian American students attend school in the West and Northeast.[9]

In spite of the diversity among Asian American groups, they are often lumped together and stereotypes about them are common. Furthermore, because of the widespread belief that all Asian American students excel academically and have positive schooling experiences, researchers and experts on multiculturalism often ignore their needs. This means that there is less published research about Asian American students than about African Americans and Latinos.[10] The experiences, contributions, and histories of Asian American groups also tend to be excluded from the K–12 school curriculum. For example, although many Americans know that Japanese Americans were forced into internment camps during World War II, most Americans—including teachers—don't know that laws were passed to prevent Asian Americans from immigrating to the United States and that Asian American students were subjected to racism and segregation in U.S. public schools. Moreover, some Asian American groups have had a much longer presence in the United States than others.

Recent arrivals to the United States, particularly immigrants who come from war-ravaged nations, are more likely than the groups with a longer historical presence in the United States to live in poverty and to have negative schooling experiences.[11] Additionally, most research about students who are English language learners focuses exclusively on Hispanic students. However, approximately 17 percent of Asian American elementary and secondary school students have difficulty speaking English, and for some groups such as Vietnamese students, the percentage is as high as 25 percent.[12]

Clearly, although Asian American students appear to thrive in public schools, upon closer inspection, depending on the group under scrutiny, the picture may look different. That's why, as a teacher, it's important for you to realize that all students, including Asian American students, need the best education that you can provide. Now, let's examine what the TC Study respondents said (see Figure 2.2).

Although we asked you to rate your confidence levels about teaching Asian American males and Asian American females separately, the TC Study respondents were only asked to rate their level of confidence about teaching Asian American students in general. Several respondents wrote comments to explain their self-ratings. Once again, a recurring theme was that teachers tended to feel more confident about working with students with whom they

Figure 2.2 What the TC Study Respondents Said About Effectively Teaching
Asian American Students

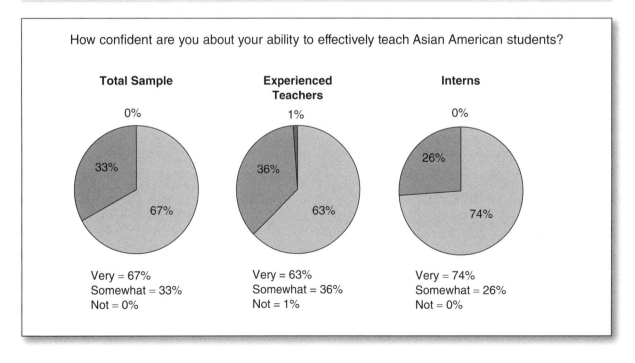

How confident are you about your ability to effectively teach Asian American students?

Total Sample

0%
33%
67%

Very = 67%
Somewhat = 33%
Not = 0%

Experienced Teachers

1%
36%
63%

Very = 63%
Somewhat = 36%
Not = 1%

Interns

0%
26%
74%

Very = 74%
Somewhat = 26%
Not = 0%

had previously worked or with students from their own racial background. A White female veteran educator said, "I've always felt pretty comfortable working with African American and Latino students and their families. I have much less confidence working with Asian American students and their families." A White male high school teacher who had taught for three years stated, "I am pretty confident with diverse groups, but have little experience with Asian Americans."

EXERCISE   What You Learned From the TC Study Respondents

1. What are the most important points that you learned from the TC Study respondents' answers?

_____

_____

_____

_____

2. Which comments differ from your views and why?

_____

_____

_____

_____

3. Which comments are most similar to your views and why?

_____

_____

_____

_____

Latinos make up the fastest growing segment of the U.S. population, and this trend is true of public schools as well. Therefore, in the next section, we'll focus on Latino students. (Note: From now on, we'll use the term *Latino* to refer to Latino males and mixed-gender groups and *Latina* to refer to Latino females.) First, please complete the following related exercise.

EXERCISE   Effectively Teaching Latino Students

1. How confident are you about your ability to effectively teach Latinos and why?

_____

_____

_____

_____

2. How confident are you about your ability to effectively teach Latinas and why?

_____

_____

_____

_____

3. Now, examine your answers and explain what you can learn from them.

_____

_____

_____

_____

WHY YOUR BELIEFS ABOUT TEACHING LATINO STUDENTS MATTER

According to the U.S. Census Bureau, "Hispanic or Latino refers to a person of Cuban, Mexican, Puerto Rican, South or Central American, or other Spanish culture or origin regardless of race."[13] In another report, the U.S. Department of Commerce revealed,

> More than half of the growth in the total U.S. population between 2000 and 2010 was because of the increase in the Hispanic population. Between 2000 and 2010, the Hispanic population grew by 43 percent, rising from 35.3 million in 2000 to 50.5 million in 2010.[14]

Just as the overall Hispanic population has grown in the United States, the same is true of the public school system. In 1990, Hispanic students accounted for 12 percent of prekindergarten–12 students. In 2010, they made up 23 percent. Therefore, "Hispanic enrollment during this period increased from 5.1 to 12.1 million students."[15] Hispanic students are more likely to attend schools in the West (40 percent), South (22 percent), and Northeast (19%) than in the Midwest (10 percent).[16] Obviously, because of their sheer numbers, as the editors of *Education Week* noted,

> [T]he economic health of the nation is tied inextricably to the educational success of this growing population. It's a matter of demographics. Latino children are the fastest-growing of the four largest racial or ethnic groups in U.S. schools. If the United States is to meet its education goals for staying economically competitive, its schools and colleges are going to have to do better by young Hispanics.[17]

Unfortunately, despite their growing numbers in the public school system, in general, Hispanic students continue to be underserved. For example, the high school graduation rate for Latinos is 63 percent, which is lower than the national average. Their average science, mathematics, and reading scores are lower than the national average, and they are more likely than White students to attend substandard schools.[18]

As a teacher, the aforementioned factors and the great likelihood that at some point in your career Latino students may constitute a substantial percentage of your students are reasons why your ability to work effectively with Latino students matters. Please keep this in mind as you read what the TC Study respondents said (see Figure 2.3) and then as you compare and contrast your responses with theirs.

Although we asked you to rate your confidence levels about teaching Latinas and Latinos separately, the TC Study respondents were only asked to rate their confidence level about teaching Latinos in general. The respondents' written

Figure 2.3 What the TC Study Respondents Said About Effectively Teaching Latino Students

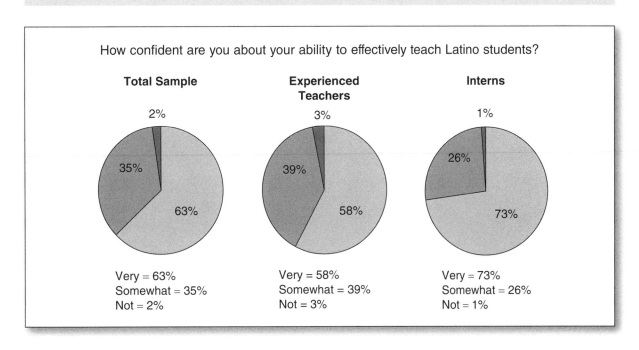

comments provide insights about their self-ratings. Once again, for some teachers, the amount of experience they had in working with specific groups of students surfaced as an influential factor. For example, an African American female elementary school teacher who had taught for more than five years said that she gave herself a *very confident* rating because of the positive results she had seen in working with certain groups of students of color. She explained,

> I am very confident teaching African American and Latino low-income students, not because of my years of experience, but because of the outcomes I have experienced, and because of the responses I received from students and somewhat from parents. Not all have been positive, but my confidence comes from the fact that I am willing to reflect and seek out answers to challenges for which I have assumed responsibility. I don't blame the kids. I believe I could successfully teach [W]hite kids, but I need proven results.

Conversely, a White female intern who had only taught for one year acknowledged, "I have some issues when it comes to teaching minority students due to my somewhat limited contact with them. There will definitely be a learning curve in my classroom, as I teach." A White male high school teacher who had taught for more than five years said, "I am less confident about racial groups I'm less exposed to."

On the other hand, several respondents insisted that they were colorblind to racial differences or that they believed that they could effectively teach any student, regardless of race. For instance, a White male high school teacher who had taught for nearly 40 years said, "I never found the kid I couldn't teach." A White female intern who had no teaching experience wrote,

> I'm confident that I can create a mindset to treat and teach all of my students respectfully and equally. Knowing that if I go into teaching, realizing that all my students are capable of learning and will learn, I can teach them all effectively. I'm confident that I have the skills to work with a diverse body of students and parents because I have the mindset to do so.

EXERCISE **What You Learned From the TC Study Respondents**

1. What are the most important points that you learned from the TC Study respondents' answers?

_____

_____

_____

_____

2. Which comments differ from your views and why?

_____

_____

_____

_____

3. Which comments are most similar to your views and why?

_____

_____

_____

_____

A NOTE ABOUT THE TERMS
BLACK AND *AFRICAN AMERICAN*

Before we ask you to rate your teaching self-confidence about working with African American students, we want you to understand that even though most people use the terms *Black* and *African American* interchangeably, the terms don't mean the same thing. *Black* is an inclusive term that, in general, refers to people of African descent. The term includes people from the Caribbean, people who live in Europe, South America, Canada, the United States, and elsewhere. However, the term *African American* usually refers to Americans of African descent whose ancestors lived in the United States before or during the American slavery era. This means that most African Americans' ancestors were slaves in the United States.

Historically, African Americans have had a very different viewpoint and set of experiences in the United States than people of African descent who *voluntarily* immigrated to America. Although we are using the term *African American* throughout this book to refer to students of African descent, please remember that Black students whose parents came to America voluntarily do not view themselves as African Americans, and these students may have different cultural practices, beliefs, and attitudes about school than African Americans. More importantly, first- and second-generation Black students from immigrant backgrounds tend to be more likely to have positive schooling experiences than African Americans whose ancestors lived in the United States during the slavery era.

The term *African American* was used on the TC Study questionnaire because after decades of school reform efforts, African American students remain more likely to have negative schooling experiences than any other group of students. Standardized test scores and school suspension and expulsion rates attest to this fact. Therefore, in the next exercise, we ask you to rate your teaching self-confidence about African American students. Then we share additional information about Black (the global term that tends to be used in many statistical reports) students in schools, followed by the TC Study respondents' self-ratings and related comments.

EXERCISE   **Effectively Teaching African American Students**

1. How confident are you about your ability to effectively teach African American females and why?

_____

_____

_____

_____

2. How confident are you about your ability to effectively teach African American males and why?

_____

_____

_____

_____

3. Now, examine your answers and explain what you can learn from them.

_____

_____

_____

_____

WHY YOUR BELIEFS ABOUT YOUR ABILITY TO EFFECTIVELY TEACH AFRICAN AMERICAN STUDENTS MATTER

In its reports pertaining to school enrollment, the National Center for Education Statistics uses the term *Black* and does not differentiate among the various groups of Black students who attend public schools. As the second-largest group of students of color in the United States, Black students account for 15 percent of the prekindergarten–12 students enrolled in public schools.[19] Whereas "from 1990 through 2010, the number of [W]hite students decreased" and the number of Hispanics increased, "the total number of [B]lack students fluctuated" and eventually "decreased from 17 to 15 percent...."[20] Black students are more likely to attend school in the South and are less likely than Whites and Asian Americans to attend school in the West.[21] In 2010, "[B]lack students had the largest share of public school enrollment in Mississippi and the District of Columbia.... Of all the jurisdictions, the District of Columbia enrolled the highest percentage of [B]lack students (77 percent)."[22]

Figure 2.4   What the TC Study Respondents Said About Effectively Teaching African American Students

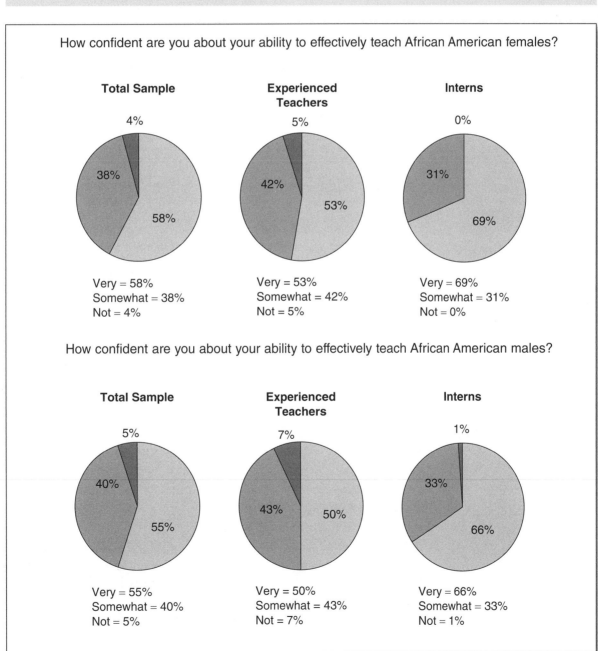

The United States has had a turbulent record in terms of race relations with people of color, but especially with African Americans. Just as institutional racism has been common in organizations throughout the nation, the same is true of schools.[23] Consequently, many African American students have had very negative schooling experiences that caused them to receive a substandard education. Therefore, as a teacher, each time that you *choose* to provide African American students and other students of color with a quality education is an opportunity to destroy a long-standing practice of inequality of educational opportunity. Figure 2.4 contains the TC Study results pertaining to African American students.

Because the gulf between teachers and African American students, especially African American males, has historically been wide, the TC Study respondents were asked to differentiate between their teaching self-confidence for African American males and their teaching self-confidence for African American females.

Several TC Study respondents wrote comments about African American students in general. For example, a White female teacher with more than five years of teaching experience said that her self-rating of *somewhat confident* about her ability to effectively teach African American students was tied to trust. She explained, "Even before [I completed] the questionnaire, I have felt only somewhat confident working with African American students because I have felt that some, not all, don't trust me." Another White female who had taught for more than five years wrote,

I am not very confident in teaching low-skill students, principally African American students, nor am I confident working with their parents. To care deeply about working with these kids and their parents, I want to get better, so that I can do something, even a little bit.

Another White female said, "I still have a lot to learn about teaching all ethnicities, but primarily African Americans, as I am currently unable to relate to them effectively at times. There are times I am able to do so." An Asian American middle school math teacher said that she felt less confident working with a specific type of African American student. She explained, "I am less confident with light [skin], high-income African Americans, but I am more confident with Latina, Asian, low-income, urban students. I prefer to work with struggling communities, and have reservations about the African American community."

Other respondents wrote specifically about either African American males or African American females. For example, a White female high school history teacher with more than five years of teaching experience admitted, "I feel pretty confident in working with all types of students, except maybe, African American females. Obviously, I feel more confident with people more like myself, but I know I can work with anyone." Regarding African American male students, a White male who had taught for more than five years said, "I am not confident when working with African

American males who are having difficulty at school. They seem to be spiraling out of control. I'm not sure how to engage the parents to help with their issues." A White female high school teacher with three years of teaching experience wrote,

> I worry that I am afraid of [B]lack students, especially boys. [They are] so boisterous, and I can't tell when a [B]lack student talks in a class, which questions/comments to respond to and which are combative. Plus [B]lack kids seem to be more argumentative, and seem to have a sense of entitlement other races lack. As for classroom management, I find my discipline incites a battle for power that I can't risk losing. Seventy-five percent of the kids I send to the Dean are African American.

In the next section, please share your thoughts about the TC Study results.

EXERCISE   What You Learned From the TC Study Results

1. What are the most important points that you learned from the TC Study results?

_____

_____

_____

_____

2. Which comments differ from your views and why?

_____

_____

_____

_____

3. Which comments are most similar to your views and why?

_____

_____

_____

_____

CONCLUSION

What We Can Learn From the TC Study

We began this chapter with two stories that were designed to remind you of an important point—when people are in need, differences don't really matter—because we wanted you to understand that all students—Native Americans, Whites, African Americans, Latinos, Asian Americans, and so on—*need* good teachers. We also asked you to complete exercises that were designed to help you take an honest look at your teaching self-confidence about teaching White students and students of color. Furthermore, we encouraged you to examine what the TC Study respondents said and to compare and contrast your self-ratings and beliefs with theirs. As you'll recall, their answers revealed the following important facts:

- The experienced teachers and the interns were more likely to say they were very confident about teaching White students than they were about teaching students of color.
- Both the experienced teachers and the interns were more likely to say they were very confident about teaching Asian American students than they were about teaching Latino and African American students.
- The experienced teachers and the interns were more likely to say they were very confident about teaching Latino students than African American students.
- Both groups were more likely to say they were very confident about their ability to effectively teach African American females than African American males.
- Experienced teachers were more likely to say that they were not confident about their ability to effectively teach African American males and African American females than they were about any other racial/ethnic group.
- A recurring theme that surfaced in the TC Study respondents' written comments was that teachers tended to feel more comfortable working with students who came from backgrounds that were similar to their own.

As a teacher, the questionnaire results contain a clear message for you: In order to become an effective teacher of all students, you can't ignore the significance of race. In fact, facing this reality will be crucial to your professional success. The advice that follows is designed to help you strengthen your relations with African American students and other students of color.

ADVICE AND STRATEGIES

1. Understand what diversity really means.

Diversity is a general term that has many meanings. For example, there's diversity among racial/ethnic groups, religions, socioeconomic status, and so on. There's also diversity *within* groups, which means that within racial/ethnic groups, students can have different background experiences, cultural practices, beliefs, personalities, religions, and viewpoints and can come from different socioeconomic statuses. An "African American" student in your class may have deep historical roots in the United States that go back to the 1600s, or an "African American" student may be a first-generation immigrant from the Caribbean or Africa. A Latino student may be a fifth-generation Mexican American or a second-generation immigrant from Columbia. An Asian American student may be a third-generation Korean American or a second-generation immigrant whose parents spent time in a refugee camp before arriving to the United States.

Because there's no way to know a student's history by looking at him/her, the best way to learn about your students' diverse backgrounds is to give them opportunities to write about, discuss, and do related presentations about their family history, culture, and their racial background through class work and homework assignments. We'll say more about this in Chapter 5, when we provide examples of standards-based, culturally relevant lesson plans.

2. Arm yourself with information about your students' racial backgrounds.

Obviously, there's no way for you to learn everything that you need to know about every single racial/ethnic group of students whom you may be assigned to teach. However, because knowledge can empower you, there are some simple ways that you can equip yourself with information that can enable you to better understand the diverse learners in your classroom and improve your lesson plans. The following examples should get you started.

The Census Bureau website (https://www.census.gov) contains reports and facts about all of the major racial/ethnic groups in the United States. If you click on the "People" heading and then the "Race" subheading, a list of "Latest Releases" about racial/ethnic groups will surface. Clicking on the "Race" subheading followed by the "Publications" subheading will allow you to access special reports and census briefs about each group.

One of the best places to find interesting and important information about racial/ethnic groups is the Smithsonian's website (http://www.si.edu). This website will allow you to access numerous cultural centers and the Smithsonian Education Center, Smithsonian Asian Pacific Center, Smithsonian Latino Center, the Anacostia Museum and Center for African American History and Culture, Smithsonian Museum of the American Indian, the Smithsonian Center for Folklife and Cultural Heritage, the National Museum of African American History and Culture, and the Smithsonian Institution Research Information System. Moreover, the website will allow you to access curriculum guides, lesson plans for K–12 students, posters, videos, reading lists, music, artwork, demonstrations, interactive exhibitions, and interviews with notable people of color.

3. Get to know yourself better.

Getting to know more about your students' racial/ethnic backgrounds and using the information to improve your relations with students of color and to strengthen your lesson plans will empower you. But getting to know yourself better is equally important. In other words, as we stated in Chapter 1, in order to become an effective teacher of all students (but especially African Americans and other students of color), you must know yourself well. What you believe—even on a subconscious level—will determine how you view and treat students. Therefore, a failure to face your true beliefs about students can backfire big time.

Because many teachers fail to do the critical personal growth work that can improve their relations with students of color, they quickly become disillusioned when things don't go as planned. For example, in *Up Where We Belong: Helping African American and Latino Students Rise in School and in Life*, I (Gail) described a first-year teacher who fit this description. This young White female teacher told me that at the beginning of the school year, she wasn't a racist. She claimed, however, that after the African American students in her class began to misbehave on a regular basis, she became a racist. I don't believe her story. What I do believe is that she was probably harboring subconscious racist views long before she entered the classroom.[24]

The first-year teacher's story illustrates that if you don't deal with your mental baggage about students of color, your baggage will surface in ways that may surprise you. Even if it's buried deep in your subconscious, what's inside of you—anger, fear, resentment, negative beliefs about students of color, and so on—will eventually surface through your actions. Therefore, to avoid a potentially embarrassing or even a racially volatile situation, it's important that you truly understand your beliefs and feelings about students of color.[25] Your responses to the previous exercises regarding your self-confidence levels about teaching Whites, Asian Americans, Latinos, and African American females and African American males are indicators of areas on which you need to work. Therefore, it's important that you use your own self-ratings to your advantage. We'll say more about this at the end of this chapter and again when we discuss classroom management.

4. Get out of your racial/ethnic comfort zone.

One of the recurring themes that surfaced in the TC Study is that many respondents said that they felt more confident about their ability to teach students who came from backgrounds that were similar to their own. Of course, this is a normal sentiment. However, because of the huge number of students of color in K–12 schools, the teacher who fails to learn how to work effectively with students from racially/ethnically diverse backgrounds is going to fail dismally. This is why we advise you to find ways to get out of your racial/ethnic comfort zone. The best way to do this is to find ways to interact with people who come from backgrounds that are different from your own. Let's examine three examples.

What Jonathan Kozol Did

Many years ago, during one of his speaking engagements that I (Gail) attended, bestselling author Jonathan Kozol explained how he constantly found ways to get out of his racial/ethnic comfort zone. Kozol, a former Boston school teacher, is Jewish, but he has spent decades exposing the ways in which African American students have historically been short-changed and even damaged by the public school system. Although he no longer teaches school, Kozol continues to spend a lot of time interacting with African American youth, including visiting their places of worship and attending events in their communities.

What Michaela Did

Michaela, the frustrated new teacher whom we mentioned at the beginning of Chapter 1, realized that attending her students' extracurricular activities could improve her relations with challenging students. For example, after she attended the basketball game of an eleventh grader who constantly broke Michaela's class rules and was often defiant and uncooperative, the girl began to behave better in class.

Attending students' extracurricular school events, places of worship, and other activities in their communities can give you opportunities to see them in a different manner; learn more about their culture, interests, and their community; and convey the message to them that you care about them. However, there are other simple ways that you can get out of your racial/ethnic comfort zone.

Talking to Strangers

Merely talking to people from racial/ethnic backgrounds that are different from your own when you see them on public transportation systems, in grocery store lines, in movie theatre lines, in airports, and on airplanes is perhaps the easiest way to get out of your racial/ethnic comfort zone on a regular basis. For example, in February 2013, I (Gail) took a trip from North Carolina to Iowa that required me to fly on three different airplanes each way. On two of the airplanes, by simply saying "hi" to the passengers who were sitting in my row, I ended up having lengthy, enriching conversations.

A Florida Keys resident, whom I met on the flight from Chicago to Iowa, shared a lot of history about the Underground Railroad stops that are located in Iowa and other parts of the Midwest. He also told me many fascinating details about Black history and "introduced" me to notable African Americans whom I'd never even heard of. When our conversation ended, he requested my business card and said that he'd e-mail me more Black history facts.

A second passenger, whom I'd greeted earlier on the Atlanta to Chicago flight, turned out to be a doctoral student and a business owner.

(Continued)

(Continued)

During the trip, this single parent of a biracial 10-year-old daughter described her dissertation study to me and explained how she planned to use it to transform the corporate workplace by making it less hostile to female employees. When the airplane landed, we agreed that our conversation had been mutually beneficial and that we would e-mail each other periodically.

Both of my fellow travelers happened to be White Americans. To me, at first glance, the Black history expert appeared to be a typical-looking middle-aged White man. But he informed me that he was a journalist who had authored many books, and during his childhood in Iowa, he had several African American close friends. His grandfather had also had close African American friends. The journalist's enduring friendships with African Americans had sparked his lifelong interest in Black history. Like the journalist, the White single mother was friendly and down-to-earth, and as we laughed and chatted on the airplane, the more we talked, the more we realized what we had in common.

Each conversation enriched me by providing me with new knowledge and reminding me that there are many similarities and common interests among people, regardless of their race/ethnicity. Additionally, the conversations made each flight seem shorter and a lot more enjoyable. The moral of these stories is this: When you encounter people from other racial/ethnic backgrounds than your own in stores, theaters, parks, airplanes, trains, buses, and so on, you never know what can happen and what you can learn if you are willing to leave your racial/ethnic comfort zone. Later, we'll discuss how your colleagues can help you get out of your comfort zone.

5. Engage in ongoing self-reflection regarding diversity.

There are no quick fixes or easy solutions to narrowing America's great racial divides. In spite of this, many teachers want to attend one workshop, read one book, or collect a bunch of handouts and believe that they've done the work that is crucial to their success with students of color. In *The Power of One: How You Can Help or Harm African American Students*, I (Gail) repeatedly emphasize that in order to work more effectively with African American students, teachers must face, address, and deal with their racial mental baggage (stereotypes, misconceptions, deficit thinking, etc.) on an *ongoing* basis.[26] This premise also holds true for teachers who want to work effectively with other racial/ethnic groups. Unfortunately, as the following story reveals, many teachers refuse to do so.

How Teachers Can Derail Progress

Many years ago, I (Gail) was invited to conduct professional development workshops for teachers in the Midwest. The equity facilitators who invited me to conduct the workshops were committed to providing K–12 public school teachers with information that was designed to increase their efficacy with African American students. The equity facilitators were enthusiastic about their work and firmly believed in its importance. Therefore, several years later, I was surprised to learn that both had voluntarily resigned from their positions. Ostensibly, burnout was the culprit, but the truth of the matter was that they grew tired and became frustrated because teachers only wanted quick fixes and eventually became resistant to their efforts. The equity facilitators concluded that most White teachers don't want to do the hard, laborious, and time-consuming work that is needed to change a lifetime of negative thinking about African Americans and other students of color.

If you truly want to become an effective teacher of all students, including African American students and other students of color, make sure that you don't adopt a craving for quick fixes, for there aren't any quick fixes or toolboxes of strategies. You *must* be willing to do the hard, painful, and ongoing work that most folks aren't willing to do. This is a major difference between effective teachers of African American students and other students of color and ineffective ones. We conclude this chapter with three strategies that can help you progress on your journey of having a great start and a great finish with African American and other students of color.

APPLYING WHAT YOU LEARNED TO YOUR *YES, I CAN!* JOURNAL

1. Create a personalized plan that will require you to leave your racial/ethnic comfort zone on a regular basis.
   a. Put the plan into practice.
   b. Record your thoughts and what you learned in your journal.
   c. Make an effort to find ways on a weekly basis to get out of your racial/ethnic comfort zone.

2. Read the following quote from a high school student who participated in a study that I (Gail) conducted.

   I am a Mexican-American girl who was born in this country. I am the first generation in this country. My family, which came from Mexico, spoke only Spanish. Growing up in a Spanish-speaking household, I did not know how to speak, read, or write English whatsoever.[27]

In your journal, explain how you would help this student thrive in your classroom.

3. Read the following works and in your *Yes, I Can!* journal, summarize your thoughts, reactions, and ways that you can use this information to increase your efficacy with students of color.

   - *The Power of One: How You Can Help or Harm African American Students* by Gail L. Thompson
   - *We Are Americans: Undocumented Students Pursuing the American Dream* by William Perez
   - *My Years as a Hispanic Youth Advocate and the Lessons I Have Learned* by Lela Lovejoy

"Oh My Gosh, He Can't Even Read!" 3

Examining Your Teaching Self-Confidence About Working With Struggling Students

MEET CORNEL: A DIFFICULT STUDENT (PART 1)

Cornel, an African American who had a strong, supportive family, is an example of one type of student who may sit in your classroom one day. His maternal grandfather was a preacher, his mother was a teacher (who later became a school principal), and his father was a hardworking college graduate. During childhood, Cornel adored his older brother, Cliff, who protected him, taught him to read, and became his main role model.

Despite the fact that Cornel was reared in a loving, supportive home environment and his parents instilled strong Christian values in their two sons, at an early age, Cornel developed an unexplainable "rage" and "restless anger."[1] By the time he was in elementary school, he was a "violent" "little gangsta" who fought other children, stole their lunch money, and lied to his teacher.[2] One day, when Cornel refused to say the Pledge of Allegiance, his second-grade teacher became enraged and slapped him. Cornel retaliated by hitting her in the arm. When the teacher left the classroom and returned with the principal, who intended to spank him, Cornel and his friends physically attacked the principal. Consequently, the principal expelled Cornel from school.[3]

Before you read Part 2 of this story, please complete the following exercise.

EXERCISE **Now It's Your Turn (Part 1)**

1. What are your initial thoughts about this story?

_____

_____

_____

_____

2. How confident are you about your ability to effectively teach a child like Cornel?

_____

_____

_____

_____

3. What would you do if one of your students refused to recite the Pledge of Allegiance?

_____

_____

_____

_____

4. In your opinion, what could cause a student who is reared in a positive home environment to become as angry and rebellious as Cornel became?

_____

_____

_____

_____

5. How do you think Cornel turned out as an adult?

_____

_____

_____

_____

MEET CORNEL:
A DIFFICULT STUDENT (PART 2)

As a result of their misbehavior at school, many students—especially Latino males and African Americans like Cornel—get pushed into the prison pipeline, which often starts with suspension and expulsion from school. Surprisingly, unlike most of these stories, Cornel's had a happy ending.

Over time, his family realized that his anger was fueled by his outrage about racism and injustice. For example, Cornel stole other kids' lunch money because he wanted to buy food for hungry students. He refused to salute the flag because he believed that it represented a country that had historically oppressed African Americans. However, after his family relocated to another state and his mother insisted that he be tested for "giftedness," Cornel was placed in a school "that was dedicated to dealing with gifted children."[4] At that school, "two loving teachers, beautiful [W]hite sisters named Nona Sall and Cecilia Angell, took [him] under their wings and taught [him] to fly."[5] Because of these factors, Cornel was able to skip fourth grade and continued to be a high achiever throughout his schooling. Today, Dr. Cornel West, who graduated Magna Cum Laude from Harvard in three years and who earned a doctorate from Princeton, is an internationally renowned professor, bestselling author, and orator.[6]

E X E R C I S E Now It's Your Turn (Part 2)

1. Now that you've read both parts of the story, what are your overall thoughts about it?

_____

_____

_____

_____

2. How can you use the messages in this story to become a more effective teacher of African American students and other students of color?

_____

_____

_____

_____

CHAPTER HIGHLIGHTS

Cornel West's story illustrates several important points. One of the main ones is that when a student, especially an African American male or a Latino, misbehaves at school, it's easy for teachers to assume that he isn't smart. So often, students like Cornel are placed in special education classes because their misbehavior is equated with a learning disability. As a teacher, when you assume that every misbehaving student should be pushed into special education or into the prison pipeline through suspension and expulsion from school, you may destroy a student's chances of having rewarding schooling experiences and a bright future. Moreover, you can cheat yourself out of the opportunity to become a "turnaround" teacher: an exemplary, life-changing educator who motivates struggling students to become academically successful.[7]

In Chapter 4, we focus extensively on how you can increase your efficacy with students like Cornel who struggle to comply with classroom and school rules. In this chapter, however, our goal is to help you become more confident about your ability to work effectively with students who struggle with course work. We begin by asking you to complete a related exercise. Next, we share research and the Teacher Confidence (TC) Study results pertaining to this topic and ask you to compare and contrast your self-ratings with those of the respondents. We conclude this chapter with advice and strategies.

EXERCISE   Examining Your Teaching Self-Confidence About Working With High Achievers

1. How confident are you about your ability to effectively teach high-achieving students and why?

_____

_____

_____

_____

2. Now, examine your answer and explain what it reveals about your teaching self-confidence level.

_____

_____

_____

_____

WHY YOUR TEACHING SELF-CONFIDENCE ABOUT WORKING WITH HIGH ACHIEVERS MATTERS

When our eldest daughter, Dr. Nafissa Thompson-Spires, started kindergarten, she already knew how to read, thanks to our work at home and the work of Sister Matthews, her outstanding preschool teacher. Sister Matthews, an African American grandmother, believed that all children need to learn to read as soon as possible and had no doubt that she was capable of teaching *all* of her preschoolers to read. Furthermore, during the year that Nafissa sat in her classroom, Sister Matthews instilled a strong love of learning in her.[8]

In spite of the fact that Sister Matthews had done an excellent job of preparing Nafissa for kindergarten, her next school year started out badly. Her kindergarten teacher was brand new, and like many first-year teachers, was extremely nervous on the first day of school. When this young White woman learned that Nafissa already knew how to read, she quickly concluded that this child didn't belong in her class. Before the first week of school ended, the teacher recommended that Nafissa be moved to a first-grade classroom. As parents, even though we were K–12 teachers ourselves at the time, we didn't realize that this was a huge mistake. In spite of the fact that our child was academically advanced, she would be nearly two years younger than her first-grade classmates. Therefore, unbeknownst to us at the time, remaining in kindergarten—even with a new and inexperienced teacher—would've been better for Nafissa than facing the peer pressure that awaited her.

Many teachers would love to teach high-achieving students like Nafissa, but as the aforementioned story suggests, some teachers would prefer not to.

Figure 3.1   How the TC Study Participants Rated Their Ability to Work With High Achievers

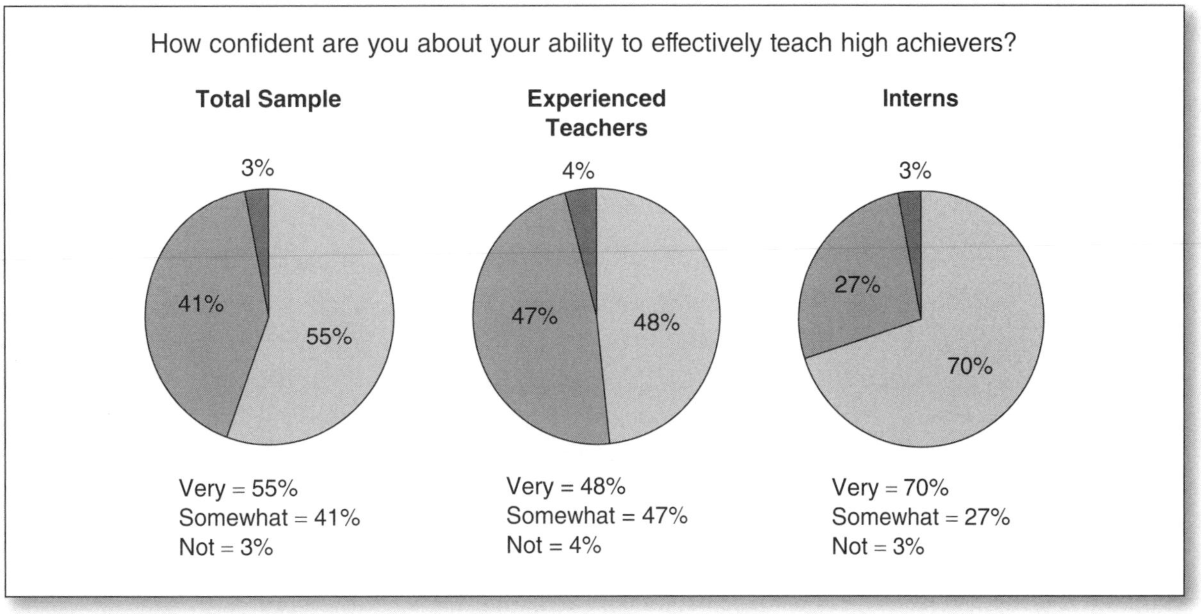

How confident are you about your ability to effectively teach high achievers?

Total Sample

3%
41%   55%

Very = 55%
Somewhat = 41%
Not = 3%

Experienced Teachers

4%
47%   48%

Very = 48%
Somewhat = 47%
Not = 4%

Interns

3%
27%
70%

Very = 70%
Somewhat = 27%
Not = 3%

Often, the reason is that teachers believe that high achievers are more demanding, more assertive, and require more teaching expertise than some teachers have or are willing to develop. Teachers who have adopted low expectations for students are very likely to fit this description, as are teachers who lack confidence about their ability to work effectively with high achievers. Nevertheless, high achievers are common in K–12 public schools nationwide, and many of these high achievers are students of color—like Nafissa or Dr. Cornel West— whose academic potential is destroyed or overlooked during their early years of school.

According to the authors of *Achievement Trap: How America Is Failing Millions of High-Achieving Students From Lower-Income Families*, there are over three million high-achieving K–12 students from lower-socioeconomic backgrounds.[9] However, the authors also explained, "Sadly, from the time they enter grade school through their postsecondary education, these students lose more educational ground and excel less frequently than their higher-income peers."[10] One of the main reasons, according to the authors, is that the "talents" of high-achieving students are "under-nurtured, similarly to the experiences of their low-achieving counterparts."[11] As a result, the authors urged educators and policy makers to pay more attention to this population of students and recommended that educators do a better job of providing these students with support, resources, and information that will increase their chances of remaining in the high-achieving category throughout their school years. Therefore, in order to become an effective teacher of all students, particularly African American students and other students of color, it's important for you to realize this and to constantly remind yourself that looks can be deceiving. In other words, it's unwise to make assumptions about a student's potential merely because of his/ her racial or socioeconomic background. Now, let's examine what the TC Study participants said about their ability to work with high achievers (please see Figure 3.1).

Several TC Study respondents wrote related comments. For example, an Asian American male intern who had no K–12 teaching experience but had taught math at the college level said, "I feel confident teaching most students of different races [and] I prefer to work with the high achieving/overachieving students." Conversely, an African American male who had taught middle school English and history for more than five years admitted that he struggled to teach high achievers. "I still don't have this GATE [Gifted and Talented Education Program] thing down," he wrote.

Although some respondents mentioned that they preferred to teach high achievers and at least one admitted that doing so was still difficult for him, instead of indicating a preference for teaching high or low achievers, several respondents emphasized that they felt more confident teaching average students. For instance, a White female intern with more than five years of teaching experience acknowledged, "I am less confident about teaching kids on the high/low spectrum of achievement." A biracial female intern who had taught high school science for one year made a similar point: "I have confidence issues with low-performing students and high-performing [students] . . . regardless of race. I may think too highly of my capabilities as a teacher." Now, we'd like for you to complete the following related exercise.

EXERCISE   What You Learned From the TC Study Results

1. What are the most important points that you learned from the TC Study results?

_____

_____

_____

_____

2. Which comments differ from your views and why?

_____

_____

_____

_____

3. Which comments are most similar to your views and why?

_____

_____

_____

_____

In the next section, we focus on low achievers in K–12 schools. First, however, we'd like for you to examine your teaching self-confidence level about working with this group.

**EXERCISE   Examining Your Teaching Self-Confidence
About Working With Low Achievers**

1. How confident are you about your ability to effectively teach low-achieving students and why?

_____

_____

_____

_____

(Continued)

(Continued)

2. How confident are you about your ability to effectively teach students who read below grade level and why?

_____

_____

_____

_____

3. How confident are you about your ability to effectively teach students who have poor math skills and why?

_____

_____

_____

_____

4. Now, examine your answers and explain what they reveal about your teaching self-confidence levels.

_____

_____

_____

_____

WHY YOUR TEACHING SELF-CONFIDENCE ABOUT WORKING WITH LOW ACHIEVERS MATTERS

Although there are millions of high-achieving students of color and high-achieving students from lower socioeconomic backgrounds in K–12 schools nationwide, there are also millions of low-achieving K–12 students from these backgrounds. As we stated in previous chapters, African American, Latino, and English language learner (ELL) students are overrepresented among the students who underperform academically and are less likely than their White and Asian American fourth- and eighth-grade counterparts to be proficient in math and in reading. Good math and good reading skills are crucial for academic success. Consequently, the authors of the *Achievement Trap: How America Is Failing Millions of High-Achieving Students From Lower-Income Families* stated,

> [I]mproving basic skills and ensuring minimal proficiency in reading and math remain urgent, unmet, and deserving of unremitting focus.

Indeed, our nation will not maintain its promise of equal opportunity at home or its economic position internationally unless we do a better job of educating students who currently fail to attain basic skills.[12]

Although struggling students deserve to have the most qualified and most experienced teachers, they are often assigned to the classrooms of new, inexperienced teachers. In a study of beginning teachers conducted by researchers at the National Comprehensive Center for Teacher Quality, 64 percent of the new teachers in "high-needs schools" who had earned their certification through "Alternate-route" teacher training programs and 41 percent of new teachers in "high-needs" schools who had gone through traditional certification programs said they were assigned to teach "the hardest to reach students."[13] Approximately 20 percent of the teachers in both groups said that they were unprepared for their first year of teaching.[14] Therefore, our goal is to ensure that you are well prepared not only during your first years of teaching, but for the duration of your teaching career. With this in mind, please see Figures 3.2, 3.3, and 3.4 and read what the TC Study participants said about their confidence levels regarding working with struggling students.

A Latina elementary school teacher with more than five years of teaching experience wrote, "I am not as confident in my ability or success at teaching various level students, such as teaching a class with abilities that vary from low achieving to high achieving." A White female high school teacher who had taught for four years wrote,

I feel conflicted about where I might be lowering standards to help more diverse classes feel successful. I perceive that the class is still challenging but am worried about whether my strategies to reach lower achievers and mid-level achievers are well conceived.

Figure 3.2 What the TC Study Participants Said About Working With Low Achievers

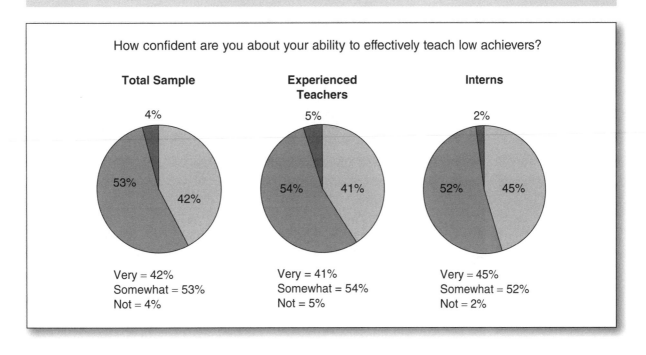

How confident are you about your ability to effectively teach low achievers?

Total Sample

4%

53%

42%

Very = 42%
Somewhat = 53%
Not = 4%

Experienced Teachers

5%

54% 41%

Very = 41%
Somewhat = 54%
Not = 5%

Interns

2%

52% 45%

Very = 45%
Somewhat = 52%
Not = 2%

Figure 3.3 What the TC Study Participants Said About Working With Struggling Readers

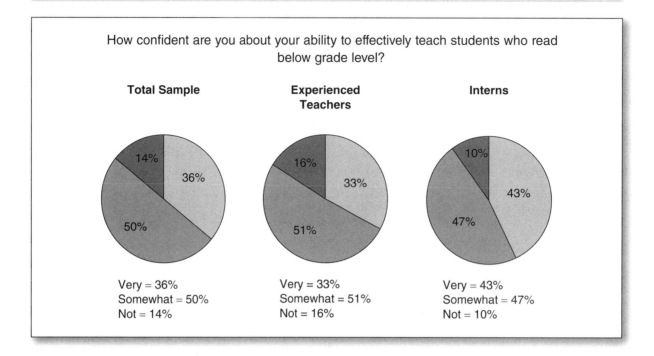

How confident are you about your ability to effectively teach students who read below grade level?

Total Sample	Experienced Teachers	Interns
Very = 36%	Very = 33%	Very = 43%
Somewhat = 50%	Somewhat = 51%	Somewhat = 47%
Not = 14%	Not = 16%	Not = 10%

Figure 3.4 What the TC Study Participants Said About Working With Students Who Have Poor Math Skills

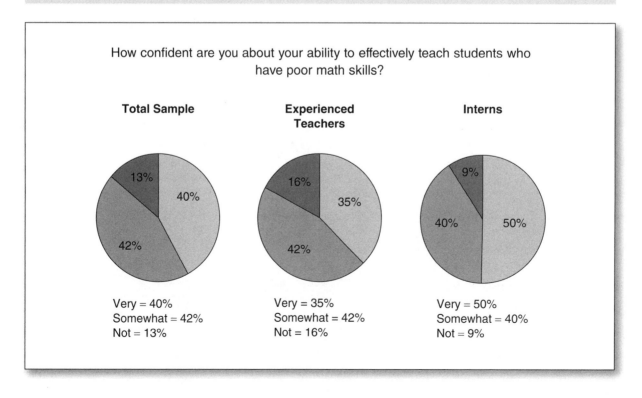

How confident are you about your ability to effectively teach students who have poor math skills?

Total Sample	Experienced Teachers	Interns
Very = 40%	Very = 35%	Very = 50%
Somewhat = 42%	Somewhat = 42%	Somewhat = 40%
Not = 13%	Not = 16%	Not = 9%

Besides working with non-English-speaking parents, the participants were less likely to feel confident about their ability to work effectively with students who were reading below grade level than any other topic that they were asked to rate. An African American female middle school teacher who had taught for more than five years stated,

> My confidence lies in my skills as a teacher. I feel I can teach all students based on race. However, I am [only] somewhat confident when it comes to low achievers that read below grade level. . . . I think this can affect their confidence in their ability to learn, as well as make me question my ability to teach.

A White high school experienced teacher admitted, "[I am] not confident in math or teaching [students] with low skills." An experienced African American female elementary school teacher said, "I don't care to teach students who cannot read or calculate math."

EXERCISE   What You Learned From the TC Study Results

1. What are the most important points that you learned from the TC Study results?

_____

_____

_____

_____

2. Which comments differ from your views and why?

_____

_____

_____

_____

3. Which comments are most similar to your views and why?

_____

_____

_____

_____

CONCLUSION

What We Can Learn From the TC Study

The TC Study revealed several important points about new and experienced teachers' confidence levels regarding working with high achievers and low achievers. The following points are worth remembering:

- Although less than half of the experienced teachers said that they were very confident about working with high achievers, the overwhelming majority of interns did.
- More than half of the interns and experienced teachers were only somewhat confident or not confident at all about their ability to work effectively with low achievers.
- Nearly 70 percent of the experienced teachers and approximately 60 percent of the interns were only somewhat confident or not confident at all about their ability to effectively teach students who read below grade level.
- Nearly 60 percent of the experienced teachers and nearly half of the interns said that they were only somewhat confident or not confident at all about their ability to effectively teach students who have poor math skills.

The TC Study results reveal that many teachers are uncertain about their ability to work effectively with high achievers and even more are concerned about their ability to work effectively with low achievers, especially those who struggle with math or reading. For these reasons, it is crucial that you arm yourself with strategies that will allow you to work effectively with these groups of students. The following strategies can help you do this.

ADVICE AND STRATEGIES

1. Remember that high achievers need good teachers.

Although it might appear that high achievers don't need the best that you have to offer, this isn't true, especially for high-achieving African American students and other students of color and high achievers from low-income backgrounds. Because these students are often overlooked and their needs are not addressed, it is easier for them to end up having negative schooling experiences than it is for high-achieving White students. In fact, being the only student of color or only one of a few students of color in Gifted and Talented Education (GATE) and Advanced Placement courses can be an extremely lonely experience for these students. Therefore, it is important for you to establish positive relationships with these students, encourage them to share their views and needs with you, and make sure that you create a safe and nurturing classroom environment for them.

2. Help struggling students change their mindsets.

Just as our goal in writing this book is to convince you that you can become a successful teacher of all students, especially African American students and other students of color, as an educator, one of your goals should be to convince your students that they can become good students. This will require you to help struggling students who may have an academic inferiority complex to start to believe that they can excel academically. Praising them often; celebrating their successes; helping them realize that a poor grade on an assignment or test does not mean that they are failures; sharing stories with them about instances when you failed at something; and allowing them to retake tests, redo assignments, and complete extra credit assignments can boost student morale and change their negative mindsets.

3. Use assessments to your advantage.

As early in the school year as possible, preferably during the first week of school, give your students an assessment (find out what is already available at your school site) to determine whether or not students possess the reading, writing, and mathematics skills that they need in order to thrive in your classroom. After you identify the specific areas in which students are struggling, develop a related action plan. For example, if a student cannot decode words, then your lesson plans should incorporate decoding strategies into them. If a student cannot comprehend grade-level reading content, then your lesson plans should incorporate reading comprehension strategies in them. If a student does not have the basic mathematics skills to excel in your classroom, then you will need to devote instructional time to teaching basic addition, subtraction, division, and multiplication skills. The same advice pertains to poor writing skills. The Appendix section of *Through Ebony Eyes: What Teachers Need to Know but Are Afraid to Ask About African American Students* contains specific reading, writing, and vocabulary-building strategies that I (Gail) used in my classroom. This information may be useful to you.

4. Make sure that you have the correct mindset about struggling students.

If you believe that struggling students will never become good students, you may subconsciously send this message to students. Therefore, it's important to constantly focus on their potential instead of their weaknesses and also to focus on your potential to help them to excel academically. In *Stem the Tide: Reforming Science, Technology, Engineering, and Math Education in America*, author David Drew stated that teachers must play a crucial role in helping students develop the skills that will enable them to become globally competitive. According to Drew, "successful education ultimately comes down to the interaction and communication between a teacher and his students."[15] Drew emphasized that in order to be effective, teachers must use a variety of strategies to reach students. Effective teachers, Drew wrote, "lead students to master and enjoy skills, techniques, and knowledge that they thought they could never acquire."[16]

5. Give struggling students the best that you have to offer.

Because it is difficult to work with struggling students and positive results may take a long time to surface, you will run the risk of becoming frustrated and engaging in the "blame game," whereby you blame students for their academic challenges and end up shortchanging them. However, if you refuse to lower your expectations, give students individualized attention when you can, allow them to work collaboratively, allow them to be assisted by their higher-achieving peers, help them understand why the subject matter is important, show them how to connect the subject matter to the real world, do frequent checks for understanding, review frequently, and encourage students to ask questions, you will be less likely to give them a second-rate education.

6. Don't reinvent the wheel.

Instead of struggling to help high achievers or low achievers in isolation, be sure to use the many ready-made materials and resources that are available to assist you. Many of these resources are on the Internet. The U.S. Department of Education website (www.ed.gov.), for example, contains lesson plans and strategies for teachers. The Reading Rockets website (www.readingrockets.org.) contains lesson plans, strategies, and other reading materials for parents and teachers. The Teachers.Net website (http://teachers.net/lessons/) contains thousands of free lesson plans for mathematics, reading, and many other subjects.

7. Know how to provide structured support to struggling students.

When you write lesson plans, you should be aware of district and school policies regarding the Multi-tiered System of Support (MTSS), whereby "needs are identified by monitoring students' progress. Adjustments to instruction and interventions are based on students' performance and rate of success."[17]

What Does the MTSS Process Look Like?

The MTSS process typically has three tiers. Each tier provides differing levels of support. It is important that you keep good records of the types and frequency of support that you provide and keep parents and appropriate school leaders informed. If an intervention becomes necessary, it will be much easier to make an informed decision if you have data on the student that clearly paint a picture of his or her achievement pattern. Those data should be based on multiple measures, including various types of assessments.

Tier I. This tier is based on the theory that your whole-group instructional practices should initially reach as many students as possible and that you should constantly be checking for understanding through formal and informal means. For example, you may have students who don't respond well verbally in class. However, to do an informal check for comprehension, you may elicit a nod from them or develop a signal, such as a thumbs-up.

Tier II. Although through high-quality instruction and an interesting and relevant curriculum, you should be able to reach most students, some struggling students will need Tier II–level support. Tier II "is aimed to provide a focused intervention for students who are not fully responding to core instruction."[18] This supplemental support consists of assistance from the teacher that exceeds whole-class instruction, typically in small groups in order to provide the remedial-skill development or other help that they need in addition to what they are receiving from the general curriculum. For example, you may work with struggling readers in small groups in order to give them more opportunities to respond to questions that are designed to determine whether or not they comprehend text, give them opportunities to ask questions, teach them how to identify the theme or main idea of a reading selection, explain the importance of rereading text at a slower pace when comprehension breaks down, and model how to use context clues instead of guessing to determine the accurate meaning of an unfamiliar word.

Tier III. Tier III–level support is for "high-risk" students, which should constitute approximately 5 percent of your students.[19] This level of support requires individualized and even smaller group support for students with the greatest needs, and their progress must be monitored frequently. For example, you may use this time to teach students who are failing to meet grade-level math standards in basic addition, subtraction, multiplication, and division rules and provide lots of opportunities for them to practice. Struggling readers may need time to learn basic phonics rules and oral reading practice in order to learn to read fluently.

APPLYING WHAT YOU LEARNED TO YOUR *YES, I CAN!* JOURNAL

1. Create an action plan that includes your goals, objectives, and several lesson plans for students who are struggling with a particular subject that you teach, such as reading, mathematics, and so on.

2. Read the following quote from a high school student who participated in a study that I (Gail) conducted.

    When I was enrolled at the . . . school, I will never forget my first day. The minute I stepped into the classroom, my heart began to beat rapidly. After I was introduced to the whole class, all I could do was remain silent because I didn't understand anything the teacher had said.[20]

In your journal, explain what you would do to help this student excel in your classroom.

3. Modify the following lesson plan for the grade level(s) that you teach and add MTSS Tier I, Tier II, and Tier III components.

A Culturally Relevant Standards-Based Lesson Plan

Grade Level: 4

Subject: Language Arts

Topic: Build a Culturally Relevant Board Game

Objective: Students will create a culturally relevant board game based on several popular games for their age group. This activity will focus on African American contributions to the United States. However, the assignment can be modified in the following ways:

- Students can create a board game that is based on Asian American contributions to the United States.

- Students can create a board game that is based on American Indian contributions to the United States.

- Students can create a board game that is based on Latino contributions to the United States.

Related Standards:

- **ELA.4.RI.3** Explain events, procedures, ideas, or concepts in a historical, scientific, or technical text, including what happened and why, based on specific information in the text.

- **ELA.4.RI.9** Integrate information from two texts on the same topic in order to write or speak about the subject knowledgeably.

- **ELA.4.W.7** Conduct short research projects that build knowledge through investigation of different aspects of a topic.

- **ELA.4.W.10** Write routinely over extended time frames (time for research, reflection, and revision) and shorter time frames (a single sitting or a day or two) for a range of discipline-specific tasks, purposes, and audiences.

Teacher Lesson Guidelines:

1. Students will play an easy, age-appropriate commercial or educational board game to orient them to the concept of individual and group play within a game situation.

2. Students will research prominent African Americans in any discipline, including athletics, politics, education, religion, and so on.

3. Students will be given the name of a prominent African American and pertinent information about the individual as the basis of the game that they will design.

4. Assessment will be based on the following:

Students will develop a board game that

- is based on factual information from texts, such as biographies and autobiographies, articles, reports, and so on;
- explains how the individual improved the United States or made an important contribution;
- includes clear and legible instructions;
- may or may not require an electric timer;
- does not require batteries;
- includes informational cards, clues, and/or images in any combination; and
- can be played in one hour or less.

Structure: Small groups

Purpose: Build understanding

Description: This activity will educate students by having them build a culturally relevant game about a prominent African American. The culminating activity will be to have another group or individual play the game.

Prep: Collect several games to use as examples.

Gather card stock and other materials necessary to build the games.

Collect biographies, autobiographies, reports, and articles about African Americans from resources, such as the Smithsonian Institute.

Materials: Paper of different weights, colors, and sizes; rulers; pencils, pens, crayons, and washable markers; dice; playing cards; dominoes

4. Read the following works and summarize your thoughts, reactions, and ways that you can use this information in the *Yes, I Can!* journal that we asked you to keep.
- *Teach Them All to Read* by Elaine McEwan
- *Overcoming Dyslexia: A New and Complete Science-Based Program for Reading at Every Level* by Sally Shaywitz
- *Multiplication Is for White People: Raising Expectations for Other People's Children* by Lisa Delpit
- *Radical Equations: Math Literacy and Civil Rights* by Robert P. Moses and Charles Cobb Jr.
- *Teaching Kids With Learning Difficulties in the Regular Classroom: Strategies and Techniques Every Teacher Can Use to Challenge & Motivate Struggling Students* by Susan Winebrenner

Part II

Student Empowerment— Teacher Empowerment

Increasing Your Teaching Self-Confidence and Your Teaching Efficacy

4 This Stuff Is Hard!

Improving Your Classroom Management Skills

MEET JAMEL: A TROUBLED STUDENT (PART 1)

Like many African American elementary school students, Jamel was an energetic little boy. He had strong leadership skills, was a gifted poet who loved to express his thoughts through rhymes, and dreamed of becoming a rapper when he grew up. But over time, Jamel's personality changed. He began to miss a lot of school, and when he did attend, he usually misbehaved. "[H]e threw erasers at teachers, tossed gum in girls' hair, [and] sliced open other children's coats so the feathers spilled out."[1]

EXERCISE　Now It's Your Turn (Part 1)

1. What are your initial thoughts about this story?

_____

_____

_____

_____

---

2. How confident are you about your ability to effectively teach a child like Jamel?

_____

_____

_____

_____

3. What would you do if one of your students threw an eraser at you?

_____

_____

_____

_____

4. What would you do if one of your students put gum in another student's hair or destroyed another student's clothing?

_____

_____

_____

_____

5. In your opinion, what could cause the personality of a student like Jamel to change for the worse?

_____

_____

_____

_____

6. How do you think Jamel turned out as an adult?

_____

_____

_____

_____

MEET JAMEL: A TROUBLED STUDENT (PART 2)

Unlike Cornel West's story, which you read in Chapter 3, Jamel's story did not have a happy ending. Whereas Cornel came from a stable and loving home, Jamel grew up in a Harlem public housing building and experienced poverty and violence throughout his childhood.

When Jamel was still in elementary school, one event changed his personality and the course of his life: His 26-year-old mother, Elaine, a single parent of four young children ranging in age from one to 10 years old, was sentenced to 20 years to life for selling four ounces of cocaine to an undercover drug agent. For a short while, Jamel and his older brother lived with their father while their two younger sisters lived with their maternal grandmother. However, after their grandmother noticed bruises on the boys as a result of brutal beatings from their father, she won custody of them. Their grandmother tried hard to keep the children on the right path and took them to visit their mother on weekends. But the prison visits were traumatic for Jamel, who cried and clung to his mother at the end of each visit. Often, the guards had to pry the hysterical child away from her legs. When health problems and financial difficulties forced his grandmother to discontinue the expensive and arduous trips to the prison, little Jamel found ways to travel from Harlem to Albany alone. "The guards were not supposed to let in children without a chaperone, but they had a hard time turning away a ten-year-old boy desperate to see his mother."[2]

At home, Jamel was soon using his strong leadership skills in other ways. After realizing that his grandmother could not afford to feed and clothe the many extended family members living in her tiny apartment, he found a way to earn money. Older drug dealers paid him to transport heroin and cocaine for them throughout the neighborhood, and "each trip to another block or another borough could earn him $100."[3] Now Jamel could not only provide food, clothing, and other comforts for the family, but he also became the family's main source of income. This heavy responsibility kept him away from home late at night and affected his school attendance. Over time, however, Jamel's deeds caught up with him, and he entered the revolving door of the prison pipeline. In prison, his giftedness and dream of being a rapper prompted him to write. During one of his many incarcerations on Rikers Island, he wrote more than 500 songs. When a governor granted his mother clemency after she served 16 years in prison, Jamel, the child who had been most affected by her absence, was serving his own prison sentence.[4]

EXERCISE   Now It's Your Turn (Part 2)

1. Now that you've read both parts of the story, what are your overall thoughts about it?

_____

_____

_____

_____

2. How can you use the messages in this story to become a more effective teacher of African American students and other students of color?

_____

_____

_____

_____

3. If you had a student like Jamel in your class, do you think that you would be able to work effectively with him or her? Why or why not?

_____

_____

_____

_____

CHAPTER HIGHLIGHTS

We hope that your answer to the question, "If you had a student like Jamel in your class, do you think that you would be able to work effectively with him or her?" was "yes" because during your teaching career, you will very likely have not only one but many students who come from challenging backgrounds like Jamel's. However, if you answered "no" or "I don't know" to the aforementioned question, rest assured that many teachers—both beginning ones and more experienced ones—feel the same way. That is why our goal in this chapter is to help you strengthen your classroom management skills and become more confident about your ability to work with students who misbehave. In addition to sharing additional information about the importance of having strong classroom management skills and explaining what the Teacher Confidence (TC) Study respondents said about classroom management, we offer specific classroom management strategies. First, however, we'd like for you to complete the following exercise.

EXERCISE   Examining Your Teaching Self-Confidence About Classroom Management

How confident are you about your classroom management skills and why?

_____

_____

_____

_____

WHY YOUR TEACHING SELF-CONFIDENCE ABOUT CLASSROOM MANAGEMENT MATTERS

Teacher morale is a big deal. In Chapter 1, you read about Michaela, a beginning teacher who taught in a high-needs school and who was frustrated because shortly before the new school year began, her principal informed her that she would be teaching eleventh grade, a grade level that she had never taught. The previous year (her first year of teaching) had been very difficult and a fistfight had even taken place in her classroom. Although Michaela was happy to have a job, she often wondered whether or not she should stick with teaching or change careers.

Many teachers, especially beginning teachers, have similar thoughts. In fact, during my (Gail's) 14 years as a K–12 teacher, I often felt the same way. In fact, I felt like quitting numerous times. There were periods when school administrators failed to provide the training and support that I needed. There were many times when students really got on my nerves, such as the year when one of my junior high school students repeatedly left nasty notes on my desk, telling me that she couldn't stand me and that I was ugly and bald-headed. Then, when I transferred to high school after teaching junior high school for three years, I had many negative experiences. In one of my eleventh-grade classes, for instance, two troublemakers nearly turned the whole class against me. Other students accused me of picking on them because of my strict classroom management style. But the worst year of all— the one when I really wanted to quit—was the 1994–1995 school year. That was the year when a rainstorm damaged my classroom ceiling and caused tiles to fall to the floor, and it was also the year when my sister died. That was also the year when a mentally ill 18-year-old Latino student, who allegedly hated "Black people," harassed me for seven months and even threatened to kill me.[5]

We shared Jamel's, Cornel's, Michaela's, and my (Gail's) stories with you in order to prepare you for reality and to emphasize what we've already told you: Teaching is a tough job, and in order to be able to work effectively with all students (especially African American and other students of color), you must arm yourself with empowering information and strategies. One of the best ways to do this is to strengthen your classroom management skills, because weak classroom management skills are a main cause of low teacher morale and one of the primary reasons why many teachers are unable to work effectively with students of color. For example, in the report *Lessons Learned: New Teachers Talk About Their Jobs, Challenges, and Long-Range Plans*, nearly half of the teachers who had received their certification through alternate routes and 41 percent of the teachers who had received their certification through traditional routes said that "a major drawback of teaching" is that "too many kids [have] discipline and behavior issues."[6]

Also, in the National Center for Education Statistics *Indicators of School Crime and Safety: 2011* report, nearly 40 percent of the public school teachers surveyed said that student misbehavior interfered with their teaching, and more than 30 percent said that "student tardiness and class cutting" interfered. However, the state or district in which a teacher taught mattered, for some teachers, such as those in the District of Columbia (59 percent) were more likely to state that student misbehavior made it difficult for them to teach.[7]

Furthermore, public (versus private) school teachers, teachers with less than 10 years of teaching experience, teachers who taught in large schools, teachers who taught in cities, and secondary school teachers were more likely to report that student misbehavior interfered with their teaching.[8] The report also indicated that only a small percentage of students ages 12–18 (4 percent) said they had been victimized at school, and approximately 11 percent of teachers said that they experienced disrespect from students "at least once a week." Additionally, "the percentage of public schools that reported widespread disorder in the classrooms decreased from 4 percent in 2007–08 to 3 percent in 2009–10." During the same years, the percentage of school officials who reported that gang activity was present also decreased to "16 percent."[9]

The fact that the majority of teachers who participated in the aforementioned studies did not report that student misbehavior interfered with their teaching should be reassuring to you. Obviously, most teachers are able to manage their classrooms well. However, it is also clear that less-experienced teachers are more likely to be adversely affected by student misbehavior. Moreover, numerous reports have revealed that teachers appear to have more difficulty working effectively with African American male students than any other group of students. School suspension and expulsion rates and school dropout rates are indicators of this problem. Also, in Chapter 2, we revealed that the TC Study respondents were less likely to feel confident about their ability to work effectively with African Americans, especially males, than they were about working effectively with White, Asian American, and Latino students. Additionally, in the Mindset Study that I (Gail) conducted for *The Power of One: How You Can Help or Harm African American Students*, the majority of the educators who participated admitted that most teachers do not treat and view African American students in the same ways that they treat and view other students.[10] These facts should increase your desire to strengthen your classroom management skills. Before we share specific strategies and explain what the TC Study respondents said about classroom management, we offer some important facts about classroom management.

Basic Facts About Classroom Management

1. Classroom management can be difficult, especially for beginning teachers.
2. Through knowledge, persistence, and determination, you can strengthen your classroom management skills.
3. No student is irredeemable.
4. It may be more difficult for you to reach certain students, especially older students, students from challenging backgrounds, and students who have had negative schooling experiences.
5. Many teachers have been successful with students with whom others have failed.
6. The most difficult students are often emotionally wounded individuals who need great teachers.

(Continued)

(Continued)

7. Great teachers can change the life course and improve the schooling experiences of students who appear to be unreachable.

8. No matter how hard you try, you may fail to reach some students, but you should never quit trying to reach them anyway.

9. Because of weak classroom management skills, many teachers push students, especially African American and Latino males, into the prison pipeline through unfair discipline practices, negative labeling, and suspension and expulsion.

10. Classroom management is directly connected to student achievement, teacher effectiveness, teacher-parent relations, teacher-student relations, teacher morale, and teacher attrition.

Now, let's examine what the TC Study respondents said about classroom management (please see Figure 4.1).

Although she had five years of teaching experience, a White educator admitted, "I do not have enough confidence to jump in, and teach and explain the rules to some of our students. By explain the rules, I mean to explain what I expect of them and what they need to do." A White male middle school teacher with more than 20 years of teaching experience wrote, "I still have more to learn about classroom management and treating all students fairly. I need to get more confidence."

In the next exercise, please summarize what you learned about classroom management from the TC Study respondents.

Figure 4.1 How the TC Study Participants Rated Their Classroom Management Skills

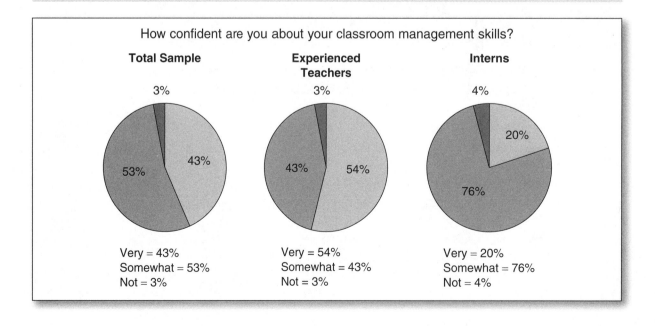

How confident are you about your classroom management skills?

Total Sample
3%
53% 43%

Very = 43%
Somewhat = 53%
Not = 3%

Experienced Teachers
3%
43% 54%

Very = 54%
Somewhat = 43%
Not = 3%

Interns
4%
20%
76%

Very = 20%
Somewhat = 76%
Not = 4%

EXERCISE   What You Learned From the TC Study Respondents

1. What are the most important points that you learned from the TC Study respondents' answers?

_____

_____

_____

_____

_____

2. Which comments differ from your views and why?

_____

_____

_____

_____

_____

3. Which comments are most similar to your views and why?

_____

_____

_____

_____

_____

CONCLUSION

What We Can Learn From the TC Study

In this chapter, we want you to understand the necessity of improving your classroom management skills, some basic facts about classroom management, and what the TC Study respondents said. Their comments and self-ratings make it clear that many teachers lack confidence about their ability to manage their classrooms effectively. Nevertheless, you do not have to be in this group of uncertain, uneasy, or ill-equipped teachers. You can develop strong classroom management skills if you empower yourself by developing effective skills and use your power to help students soar academically instead of pushing them into the prison pipeline. Empowering yourself requires that you face and deal with any negative beliefs that you have about students, that you strengthen your assertiveness skills, and that you arm yourself with useful strategies. The following strategies and professional growth exercises will help you improve your classroom management skills and will thereby enable you to work more effectively with all students, especially with African American students and other students of color.

ADVICE AND STRATEGIES

The advice and strategies that follow will help you strengthen your classroom management skills. As you are reading them, please remember to keep the following points in mind:

- A good classroom management system is built on relationship building between teachers and their students.
- Each teacher has to develop a classroom management style that suits his or her personality type. For example, I (Gail) am a strict, no-nonsense person. Therefore, some of the strategies that I recommend may not be viewed as useful to an educator with a different type of personality.
- Only use the strategies that you deem appropriate.

Today, many school leaders are focusing on positive classroom management strategies with the goal of keeping students in class as much as possible. Therefore, referrals to the office and suspension should only be used as last resorts or if you or other students are in danger.

Some educators view discipline strategies—such as having students write standards, write letters of apology, or conduct research projects as we later recommend—as punitive and counterproductive. However, I (Gail) found these strategies to be quite useful and viewed them as a way to actually strengthen students' basic writing skills rather than give them a negative impression of writing. I also recently observed that an outstanding African American elementary school principal also used the letter of apology as an effective and humane discipline strategy. If you have a problem with the notion of assigning writing as a disciplinary strategy, then replace it with one that is more suited to your beliefs and personality.

1. Remember the most important thing.

A teacher once asked me (Gail) a very profound question: "What is the most important thing that teachers need to know about educating African American students?" My answer was simple, "Treat them as you would want your own flesh-and-blood relative to be treated."[11] This sounds simple. After all, it's merely a variation of the timeless Golden Rule. However, I've learned that for many teachers, it's much easier to say this than to do it.

A good example is a little story that a White veteran educator in northern Iowa shared with me (Gail) in 2013. She said that a soft-spoken young White teacher came to her for advice. The teacher was disturbed that an African American teacher had told her that because of her soft voice, she would fail with African American students. "You have to yell at them!" the other teacher insisted.

Even though it wasn't the first time that I had heard this erroneous belief, the story saddened the veteran teacher and it angered me. Although many teachers believe this stereotype, it is actually a dangerous and destructive way to treat children, and it can backfire. Yelling at a student is a weak classroom management skill that may prompt a troubled student to become combative. Conversely, speaking to and treating students in a respectful manner is one of the best ways that teachers can earn students' respect. Using a firm voice is important when requesting that students comply with class rules; using a disrespectful tone is unwise. If you would not automatically assume that it is okay or necessary to yell at White students—especially those from upper-class backgrounds—then don't assume that it is acceptable to yell at African American, Latino, or Asian American students either, especially if they come from low-income backgrounds!

2. Be prepared on the first day of school.

When students arrive in your classroom on the first day of school, make sure that you explain your class rules to them verbally and in writing. Your class rules should be simple and clear. They should also be realistic and student centered. For example, during my (Gail's) years as a K–12 teacher, my class rules were

- be prepared (which meant that students should come to class with pencils, paper, homework, the textbook, etc. Students who could not afford to purchase writing materials were informed on the first day of school that I would provide these materials for them if they came to me after school and requested them.),
- be prompt (which meant that I expected students to be in their assigned seats before the bell rang instead of scrambling to their desks when the bell rang), and
- be an active participant (which meant that I wanted students to engage in all class activities: independent work, group work, class discussions, etc.).

After you explain your class rules to students, give them a written document that includes your expectations, grading policy, grading scale, and missed- or late-work policy. This document should contain lines for the students' and parents' signatures and the date. In my (Gail's) case, I offered an extra credit incentive for students who returned the signed document by the end of the first week of school and kept the signed documents in a file cabinet in my classroom. Posting the class rules in your classroom is also a good idea.

3. Understand what being fair really means and the importance of treating students fairly.

Treating students fairly is not the same as treating all students equally. You won't be able to treat all students equally and have positive results. They arrive at school with different experiences, and those experiences can affect their classroom behavior. It is also important to realize that many teachers who believe that they treat African American and other students of color fairly actually engage in offensive and even racist behaviors. For example, these teachers use a babyish or condescending voice that suggests that they believe that the students cannot comprehend them if they communicate in the way in which they would speak to White students. Furthermore, teachers often overreact to seemingly innocent or normal childish behaviors—such as giggling, sneezing, passing notes, gum chewing, talking to another student, or talking out of turn—by African American students and other students of color and use these behaviors as excuses to send them to the principal's office. Another widespread and unfair practice to which teachers often subject students of color is giving them boring, watered-down assignments that stem from low expectations and an innate belief in the intellectual inferiority of African American students and other students of color. This is a great way to encourage students to misbehave.

4. Use your authority wisely.

Being the main authority figure in the classroom puts you in a very powerful position. If you are having a bad day or you have been asked the same question several times and are fed up, don't take it out on the next student who asks the same question. Sometimes, it pays to take a step back and make sure that you are meeting simple protocols for treating students fairly. As you deal with students, try to put yourself in their shoes whenever possible. Remember that you weren't perfect when you were a child and that it's unrealistic to expect students to be perfect.

5. Hold yourself accountable for improving your classroom management skills.

As we stated previously, strengthening your classroom management skills will require hard work and persistence. It will also require a willingness to learn from less-than-ideal situations, especially those that appear to go badly, and to hold yourself accountable on a regular basis. Writing the following questions in your *Yes, I Can!* personal growth journal and answering them periodically is a simple way to hold yourself accountable for continuing to work on your classroom management skills:

Personal Accountability Questions

a. How well do I handle most disruptive behaviors in my classroom?

b. How much time am I spending on classroom management each day versus time on instruction?

c. Which student(s) tends to violate my class rules most frequently and why?

d. Are the disruptive students really more disruptive than others or am I focusing more of my attention on the so-called disruptive ones in order to catch them in the act of misbehaving?

e. Do I treat and view students who have been disruptive in the past in a fair and respectful manner when they are complying with class rules?

f. Do I tend to overreact when a student of color misbehaves more often than when a White student behaves in the same manner?

g. Do I give the same exact consequences to White students who engage in the same misbehaviors as African American students and other students of color whom I penalize?

h. Do I tend to say nice things to certain students and not to others?

6. Use a teaching style and teaching strategies that decrease the likelihood that students will become disruptive.

Boredom is one of the main reasons why students may misbehave in class, so make sure that you use interesting and relevant lesson plans. If you choose to lecture for long periods of time, expect for students to become disruptive. If you insist that students sit quietly for long periods of time, expect trouble. If you rarely allow students to collaborate or share their viewpoints and experiences and if you spend the bulk of your instructional time drilling them to pass standardized or other types of tests, many students (especially African American students, students of color from challenging backgrounds, and low-income students) will become apathetic, disruptive, and possibly even resentful.[12]

7. Use a Preemptive Discipline Model.

During my (Rufus's) years as a middle school teacher, my mentor, Rand Shumway, who was an outstanding teacher and school principal, taught me the concept of what I call *Preemptive Discipline*. The idea is to find students doing something—no matter how insignificant it may be—that is positive and contact the students' parents the first week or two of the school term. Telephone the parent or send a note home in order to inform the parent about the student's positive behavior. Placing a special note in the student's folder on colorful notepaper or stationary makes a huge difference when parents come for parent-teacher conferences, Back-to-School Night, or Open House. In other words, using a Preemptive Discipline Model means that you will not wait until something negative occurs before you contact the parent. Sharing positive news with parents is a great way to improve your relations with them.

Furthermore, using a Preemptive Discipline Model is a simple way to improve your relations with students—those who are disruptive as well as quieter, well-behaved ones. Disruptive students may be used to teachers sending negative news to their parents. Knowing that you are sending positive news can change their outlook and their behavior. On the other hand, teachers are less likely to contact the parents of certain students, especially the quiet ones. Often, these students do what they are supposed to and consciously remain under the radar to avoid embarrassment and perceived humiliation. Consequently, their parents rarely receive any feedback on report cards or during conferences except "Clarinda is doing just fine." However, the quiet students may secretly wish that you would say more. After telephoning their parents, I have actually had dozens of these students walk into my classroom, cover their mouths, and whisper to another student, "Mr. Thompson called my mom and told her I am a quiet leader." Then they would look back and smile or roll their eyes and maybe even nod their head in approval. Sometimes the parents would tell me by telephone, in person, or by letter that they had never, ever, heard anything positive about their child and thank me.

8. Use your two ears as a classroom management empowerment tool.

One of the main reasons why teachers disproportionately punish certain students of color, such as African Americans and Latinos, is that they claim that these students are more likely to be disrespectful by talking back and challenging what the teachers say. However, in their failure to listen carefully to what the students and their parents have to say and to ascertain the reasons why the students are challenging them, the teachers fail to learn information that could help them improve their classroom management skills and their relations with these students. Students who are assertive and who have high self-esteem are often the ones whom teachers with weak classroom management skills attempt to destroy through biased and overly punitive discipline practices. In fact, as our three children were matriculating through the K–12 school system, there were a few times when they came close to being damaged by teachers who refused to listen to their concerns.

A good example is an experience that our middle child had in third grade. Unfortunately, unlike her previous teachers, her third-grade teacher believed that students should be seen and not heard and that the classroom should be as quiet as a library. Although the teacher was strict and believed that students needed to spend several hours working on homework each night, we still hoped that our daughter would have a good school year. During the first week of school, however, our child came home in tears because her teacher had marked up her paper with red ink. To our surprise, the teacher had even corrected the way that our daughter had written her name: NaChe' (pronounced Nashay).

Well, my (Rufus's) blood started to boil. I pondered how I was going to deal with this teacher at this point and fought the urge to become an angry Black man. After pacing around and consulting Gail, I decided to write a note to the teacher and attach it to the blood-stained-looking worksheet. In my note, I emphasized that NaChe' had learned to spell her name when she was two years old and that as a toddler, she knew her parents' names and her telephone number. In fact, in order to teach our children how to spell their names, I taught each one a special song. Furthermore, when she started kindergarten, NaChe' already knew how to read and write. Therefore, as a concerned parent, I felt it necessary to correct this teacher before she damaged our child and labeled her a discipline problem. My strategy worked. The teacher got the message but never warmed up to us.

As a teacher, you can avoid making the mistake that the third-grade teacher made. If you are unclear about the spelling or pronunciation of a student's name, then simply ask the child and ask the parent! What you want to be careful of is placing students of color in stereotypical categories based on your perception of their condition. Preemptive discipline helps you understand the culture. Even if you are a teacher of color, the institutional racism model can unknowingly prejudice you against African American students and other students of color. Sometimes just asking simple questions about the correct way to spell or say a student's name can alleviate potential problems, if you are receptive to receiving feedback.

9. Use a rewards system.

Another way to practice Preemptive Discipline is to reward students for good behavior. Most individuals, regardless of their age, enjoy receiving rewards. During my (Rufus's) years as a middle school teacher, I borrowed an idea from a master teacher whom I observed and, consequently, created my own rewards system. I simply placed photos of our three children on sheets of paper that were cut to the size of a dollar bill, placed the child's photo in the middle, added a value to the fake money (such a $1, $5, or $10), and called it "Thompson Bucks." I used the currency to reward students and also to discipline them, in order to teach them the consequences of making poor choices.

The way the system worked is that each day as I was teaching, I would find ways to reward students for doing things based on themes. Rather than putting names on the board or pulling cards, I would give out Thompson Bucks, sometimes to the whole class, based on the themes addressed that day. Because I taught several social studies classes, I would put the students in social situations and reward them for demonstrating "social graces."

For example, one day, we were working on the proper way to greet someone with respect after covering a lesson on the history of England. I asked the students to address their classmates and friends that day as "Mr." or "Miss" and by their last names. Then I gave them the lowest value Thompson Buck for that day. The next day, I gave Thompson Bucks to students who participated in the class discussion. When students were acting out, I would use appropriate discipline, but instead of singling out their behavior, I would reward cooperative students and not the ones who misbehaved. Several times throughout the school year, I would have auctions, whereby students could use their Thompson Bucks to bid on inexpensive items, such as school supplies, books, and toys that I had purchased. The highest bidder would win. My discipline problems nearly disappeared. Yes, there were still discipline problems, but they were minimal. Some of my former students (who are adults now) still contact me today and talk about the auctions!

10. Educate yourself about fear.

One of the best ways to improve your classroom management skills and work more effectively with all students (but especially African American students and other students of color) is to educate yourself about fear and know the difference between rational and irrational fear. Fear is a normal human emotion, and everyone is fearful of something. There are times when fear is a logical response, and there are times when fear may be unwarranted.

Because of racism and stereotypes from the media, history, family members, and peers, most Americans are conditioned, starting in childhood, to fear African Americans. Research has repeatedly shown that the majority of African Americans are law-abiding citizens, yet many individuals—including educators—cling to an illogical fear of African Americans.

The key is to have balance. While it is important not to engage in behaviors that stem from stereotypes and unwarranted fear, it is also important to be self-protective. A good way to achieve this balance is to know the characteristics of a potentially dangerous student. According to Gavin De Becker, an expert on violence, warning signs that can protect you from violence include the following:

- "inability to control impulses"
- unrealistic need for recognition
- lack of empathy
- frequent or extreme anger
- substance abuse
- idolizing serial killers
- a history of harming animals
- a fascination with "graphic violence" in music, art, books, and so on
- a fascination with weapons
- "threatening and attempting suicide"
- "threatening homicide"[13]

If a student displays any of the above behaviors, contact the school psychologist, school counselor, other school administrators, and social services agents. Do not allow yourself or your other students to be placed in dangerous situations, and do not underestimate the student's potential to become violent. Furthermore, do not meet with the student without another adult being present.

11. Don't punish truth tellers.

One of the main reasons why America has not progressed further in terms of race relations is the fact that truth tellers have historically been denigrated, marginalized, and demonized. Dr. Martin Luther King Jr. was a classic example. Even though Dr. King advocated nonviolence and used nonviolent strategies to improve race relations, many Americans—including members of the clergy—viewed him as a troublemaker. Consequently, he was murdered.

In classrooms, outspoken students of color are often penalized by unassertive teachers who fear them. Conversely, wise teachers will choose to listen to what the students are saying and will use what they learn to improve their classroom management skills and their instructional practices. For example, instead of punishing a student for complaining that classwork is boring, you can ask, "If you were the teacher, how would you make this lesson more interesting?"

12. Include attention-getting strategies in your classroom management system.

A good classroom management system includes ways to get students' attention when necessary. Often, after students have been working in groups or with a partner, they want to continue to engage in conversations with their classmates. This makes it difficult for the teacher to regain control. Therefore, it is important that you include attention-getting strategies in your classroom management system. Yelling should not be an option, and if you have already earned your students' respect, you will find that simple actions, such as the following, will suffice.

When I (Gail) taught high school, I would merely flip the light switch back and forth to let students know that it was time to return to their seats, settle down, and give me their undivided attention. When I (Rufus) taught middle school, one of my colleagues used a verbal system with her students. She would say "Bop, bop, bop," and the class would say the same thing in response. They knew that this meant that she wanted their attention. On the other hand, I (Rufus) used the thumbs-up method. I would hold my thumb up, and my students would do the same thing, until every student eventually settled down. We urge you to find a signal that works for you, inform your students early in the school year what the signal means, and then use it consistently.

13. Strengthen your relationships with students.

Many researchers have emphasized that good teachers form strong, positive, professional relationships with their students. This is also an effective classroom management strategy, because teachers who have developed a rapport with their students and whom students respect are less likely to have serious discipline problems in their classroom. The following strategies can assist you in strengthening your relationships with African American students and other students of color:

Simple Relationship-Building Strategies

- View students as humans who have strengths, weaknesses, goals, and dreams just as all humans have.
- Remember that they possess knowledge and cultural capital that can be beneficial to you.
- Treat them respectfully.
- Apologize when warranted.
- Keep healthy boundaries.
- Smile.
- Compliment and praise them.
- Help natural leaders hone their leadership skills.

Furthermore, understanding what African American and other students of color need from you can also make it easier for you to build positive, professional relationships with them. The following list contains examples of some of these needs.

What African American Students and Other Students of Color Need From You

- For you to realize how powerful you are

- A commitment from you to use your power to help them rather than to harm them

- For you to face and address any mental baggage that you have about them

- For you to have a positive perspective of them

- For you to keep in mind that even though America has "stepchildren" (individuals who are deemed as less deserving), every child is gifted and talented

- Advice and strategies that will help them succeed academically

- Help in identifying their strengths

- For you to genuinely care about them

- Encouragement

- For you to be a positive role model

- Help in dealing with their issues, weaknesses, and so on

- Conflict resolution skills

- For you to push them toward college instead of toward prison

- For you to do everything within your power to help them receive an outstanding education

- For you to understand who they are, what they need, and why they behave the way that they do

- For you to remember the Golden Rule when interacting with them

14. Consider using (and modifying) the following three strategies to deal with students who are verbally disrespectful.

First Offense: Sample Script to Use With a Student Who Has Been Verbally Disrespectful to You

Note: Use a firm voice and look directly into the student's eyes. Replace Jamel's name with that of your student. If the student has disrespected another student instead of you, the teacher, then have him/her write the letter of apology to the other student. All writing assignments—letters of apology and standards—should be written in the student's own handwriting and should not be written during class time. **Also, make sure that you document everything, keep good records, and notify the student's parent or guardian *each* time an offense occurs.**

Jamel:

    I would like to speak with you outside.

    (After the student steps outside, stand in the doorway, so that you can keep an eye on the rest of the class [if you don't have an instructional aide] and also give the disrespectful student privacy. Asking him/her to step outside is a great way to keep the situation from escalating and a way to allow the student to save face instead of being embarrassed in front of his/her classmates.)

    Jamel, I asked you to step outside because your comment (or tone or language) was inappropriate, disrespectful, and unacceptable.

    Can you explain why you behaved in this manner?

    I appreciate the fact that you explained your reason(s) to me. However, there are always consequences for misbehavior. In this case, there will be two. I will notify your parent or guardian about this incident, and I also want you to write a letter of apology to me. In your letter, explain what you did, why it was inappropriate, and how you plan to prevent this from happening in the future.

    The letter is due tomorrow. It should be neat and free of errors. Sign it, add the date, and also have your parent or guardian sign and date it. After I read it, I will make several copies of it: one for your counselor, one for the assistant principal (or dean of discipline), and one for my file.

    Do you have any questions?

    Please return to your seat and finish your class work.

Second Offense

Note: The standards should not be written during class time. Instead of using a word processor and simply copying and pasting the standards, the student should be required to write them in his or her own handwriting. If your teaching style or academic setting does not allow for this type of discipline, substitute an appropriate consequence of equal effect.

Understand that discipline is not supposed to feel good but should be effective. Also, consider what precipitated the student's behavior in the first place. If you enabled the student and the result was the behavior you witnessed or that was reported to you, then punishing a student who reacted negatively to something that you did will have a negative effect regardless of the discipline strategy that you use.

If a student verbally disrespects you (or a classmate) a second time, in addition to using the letter of apology strategy, you can require the student (depending on his/her age and grade level) to write 50–500 standards. If the victim is another student, substitute the word *classmate* in lieu of *teacher* and add the classmate's name at the beginning of the script. The parent or guardian's signature should be required, the date must be included, and copies should be given to the student's counselor and assistant principal (or dean of students); make sure that you keep a copy for your records.

Sample Writing Standards to Assign to a Verbally Disrespectful Student

Ms. (or Mr.) (add your name) is my teacher. My teacher deserves to be treated respectfully at all times. From now on, I will behave in class, follow directions, and treat my teacher and my classmates respectfully.

Third Offense

In addition to writing another letter of apology and more standards than the number previously assigned, repeat offenders should be required to conduct research projects (on their own time) that will be presented to the entire class regarding (a) why profanity or sexist, racist, or demeaning language is inappropriate; (b) how they would feel if someone disrespected them or one of their loved ones; (c) why it is inappropriate to behave in a disrespectful manner toward others; and (d) definitions and examples of *respect*. The student's parent or guardian should sign the report or project, and copies should be given to the aforementioned school officials.

Additional Offenses

If a student continues to use offensive language in your classroom after you have tried numerous strategies, request a meeting with the parent, the student, and at least one school leader. Take your evidence (the strategies that you used to try to get the student to behave) to that meeting, and share it with the parent and school leaders. First, try to develop an action plan with the group. The plan should include expected behaviors, consequences, and a time line. If the action plan fails to work and the student continues to be disruptive, at this point, you should feel free to request that the student be removed permanently from your class on the grounds that a chronically disruptive student robs you and other students of valuable instructional time. Unfortunately, this is sometimes an alternative that teachers have to consider, for no teacher should be forced to be subjected to disrespect, abuse, or barriers to teaching on an ongoing basis. In a democratic society, teachers should also have rights. Make sure that you do your best to create a strong classroom management system, but when your relationship-building strategies and other strategies fail to reach a disruptive student, take a stand for yourself and for your other students! In the long run, standing up for yourself and your other students may differentiate you from the teachers who quit early and put you in the category with those who ended up having a long, rewarding, and productive teaching career.

APPLYING WHAT YOU LEARNED TO YOUR *YES, I CAN!* JOURNAL

1. Reread the "Jamel: A Troubled Student" story at the beginning of this chapter. Pretend that Jamel is a student in your class.
   a. Make a list of strategies that you could use to help him comply with your class rules.
   b. Make a list of options that you could use if he threw an eraser at you.
   c. Make a list of options that you could use if he damaged another student's clothing.
   d. Make a list of strategies that you could use to develop a strong, positive professional relationship with Jamel.

2. Read the following quote from an Asian American high school student who participated in a study that I (Gail) conducted.

   > My first day of school was not what I had expected. I was frightened to death and I dreaded the thought of not having my sister and brothers around. I thought I looked different from everybody else. I had slanted eyes and they had big round eyes with yellow hair. Some people treated me nice, while others laughed and mocked me.[14]

   In your journal, explain how you would help this student excel in your classroom.

3. Read the following works and, in your journal, summarize your thoughts, reactions, and ways that you can use this information.
   - *A Handbook for Teachers of African American Children* by Baruti K. Kafele
   - *Kill Them Before They Grow: Misdiagnosis of African American Boys in American Classrooms* by Michael Porter
   - *Invisible No More: Understanding the Disenfranchisement of Latino Boys and Men* edited by P. Noguera, A. Hurtado, and E. Fergus
   - *Skin Color and Identity Formation: Perceptions of Opportunity and Academic Orientation Among Mexican and Puerto Rican Youth* by E. Fergus
   - *Students Who Drive You Crazy: Succeeding With Resistant, Unmotivated, and Otherwise Difficult Young People* by Jeffrey A. Kottler
   - *Changing School Culture for Black Males* by Jawanza Kunjufu

5 A Recipe for Success

Effective Instructional Practices

ANOTHER STUDENT FROM A CHALLENGING BACKGROUND (PART 1)

During his childhood, Lloyd Dean had many strikes against him. First, he was an African American male who was born into a society that had a long, negative reputation with African American males. Furthermore, "his father was a foundry worker and his mother was a homemaker. For years, the family was on and off welfare. They had no health insurance [and] the first time [Lloyd] visited a doctor was when he was in junior high school."[1] On top of this, his father had a bad temper, and Lloyd feared him. Often, his father took his frustration out on his children, and when Lloyd looked at the lives of other adults in his community, he realized that "broken dreams" were common.[2]

EXERCISE   Now It's Your Turn (Part 1)

By now, you know that during your teaching career, numerous students from challenging backgrounds will probably be assigned to your classroom. You also know that you can use these opportunities to change the direction of a student's life and increase his or her chances of having a bright future. So we'd like for you to pretend that Lloyd was one of your students and answer the following questions:

1. In your opinion, how did Lloyd behave at school?

_____

_____

_____

_____

2. If Lloyd were one of your students, how do you think you would treat him?

_____

_____

_____

_____

3. If Lloyd were one of your students, what specific strategies would you use to help him succeed in your classroom?

_____

_____

_____

_____

4. Based on the limited information that we shared with you about Lloyd's life, how do you think he turned out as an adult?

_____

_____

_____

_____

ANOTHER STUDENT FROM A CHALLENGING BACKGROUND (PART 2)

Although he had a very difficult childhood, Lloyd had several factors working in his favor. First, in spite of the fact that his father usually earned less than $10,000 each year to support his wife and nine children and had a temper that Lloyd feared, Lloyd's parents emphasized the importance of a good education. Second, Lloyd also had a sympathetic sixth-grade teacher who cared about him. Once, she even gave him a coat to protect him from the winter cold. These positive factors prompted Lloyd to earn good grades and become an outstanding student. Consequently, he became the first person in his community to go to college, earned a bachelor's degree in sociology and a master's degree in education, and became a junior high school teacher and a part-time university instructor. If Lloyd's story ended here, the ending would still be a happy one. But there's more to his story.

Throughout Lloyd's life, his strong leadership skills were apparent to many observers. Because of this, he often received nonteaching job offers that he usually turned down. Lloyd loved teaching and was happy with his salary. Over time, however, he accepted a lucrative offer to enter the corporate world. Consequently, today, as the CEO of a nonprofit health care organization, Lloyd has earned the reputation of being one of the nation's most respected business leaders. Hallmarks of his leadership style include taking a sincere personal interest in people, speaking in a direct manner, being fair, and being diplomatic. His hard work and credibility as a leader have also resulted in personal success: Lloyd has been married for nearly 40 years and he is a multimillionaire.[3]

EXERCISE   Now It's Your Turn (Part 2)

Now that you have read both parts of the story, what can you learn from it that can help you work more effectively with African Americans, other students of color, and students from challenging backgrounds?

_____

_____

_____

_____

CHAPTER HIGHLIGHTS

So far, three of the stories that you've read have been about African American males: Lloyd Dean, Jamel, and Cornel West. Although each of these individuals could have stayed on a negative life course, Lloyd Dean and Cornel West ended up becoming extremely successful in life. In both cases, teachers had a positive impact on them, and both became educators. In previous chapters, we explained why it's important for you to strengthen your classroom management skills and to build your confidence levels about working with all types of students, especially African American students and other students of color. In this chapter, our goal is to help you to become an outstanding instructional leader of all students, specifically African American students and other students of color. Before we delve deeply into this topic, the following characteristics that contributed to Lloyd Dean's success as a junior high school teacher and later as a CEO are noteworthy, because they should become characteristics of your teaching career.

Basic Facts About Instructional Leaders Based on Lloyd Dean's Characteristics

- Strong leadership skills
- Determination
- Sincere personal interest in others
- Speaking in a direct manner
- Fairness
- Being diplomatic
- Hardworking
- Credibility
- Love teaching

Now, we'd like for you to complete a related exercise.

EXERCISE Examining Your Teaching Self-Confidence About Effective Instructional Practices

1. Which of the nine characteristics that contributed to Lloyd Dean's success as an educator and as a CEO do you possess?

_____

_____

_____

_____

2. Which of the nine characteristics do you need to develop or strengthen?

_____

_____

_____

_____

(Continued)

(Continued)

3. How knowledgeable are you about the subject(s) that you are supposed to teach?

_____

_____

_____

_____

4. How confident are you about your ability to explain your subject matter to all students, including struggling students and students of color and why?

_____

_____

_____

_____

5. How confident are you about your ability to create effective lesson plans?

_____

_____

_____

_____

WHY EFFECTIVE INSTRUCTIONAL PRACTICES ARE IMPORTANT

Like Lloyd Dean, most teachers love teaching. In fact, in *Lessons Learned: New Teachers Talk About Their Jobs, Challenges, and Long-Range Plans*, nearly half of the beginning teachers said that "putting underprivileged kids on the path to success" was one of the main reasons why they became teachers, and 44 percent said that "teaching a subject that [they] love[d] and getting kids excited about it" was one of the main reasons why they chose to teach.[4] Nevertheless, in spite of their love for teaching, many teachers—especially beginning teachers—struggle to help students learn the curriculum. In fact, in the same *Lessons Learned* report, 34 percent of the beginning teachers said that for them, the number of unmotivated students was a "major drawback" to teaching, and 42 percent said that because of the amount of testing that is required, they do not have "enough freedom to be creative."[5]

Although subject matter competency is vital, knowing how to convey that information to students, especially to struggling students and students who have historically underperformed on standardized tests, is a problem that continues to plague the teaching profession. Before we describe a successful beginning teacher and explain what a group of students of color said about effective and ineffective instructional strategies, let's first examine what the Teacher Confidence (TC) Study respondents said.

WHAT THE TC STUDY RESPONDENTS SAID

Despite the fact that the questionnaire did not contain a specific statement requiring the respondents to rate their teaching self-confidence about their ability to teach their subject matter or to create effective lesson plans, several TC Study respondents wrote related comments on their questionnaires. Some, such as the White intern who had worked at a school for more than five years as an instructional aide (but had not started teaching in her own classroom yet) were confident. According to this woman, "I have no problem teaching students of different races, nor [do I] lack confidence in my teaching skills." Others, such as a Latina who had no teaching experience, were less confident. She wrote, "I am somewhat confident in my teaching abilities. I am in the middle [because] I have no real teaching experience, and don't really know what to expect." A Latino intern who had taught elementary school for one year admitted, "I'm confident in teaching students I feel I can relate to or help [but] I'm not confident teaching students I can't relate to." A White male beginning high school teacher explained, "I feel my lack of confidence comes from my lack of experience, not lack of ability. First year is tough enough but incorporating different skills for different groups . . . ain't easy." An Asian American female who had taught high school for more than five years said, "I'm in need of skills, strategies, [and] awareness. I'm confident in my ability and desire to relate to students of color, but not terribly confident in how I address their academic needs."

EXERCISE What You Learned From the TC Study Respondents

1. What are the most important points that you learned from the TC Study respondents' comments?

_____

_____

_____

_____

(Continued)

(Continued)

2. Which comments differ from your views and why?

_____

_____

_____

_____

3. Which comments are most similar to your views and why?

_____

_____

_____

_____

One of the best ways to learn how to become an effective instructional leader of all students, but especially of students of color, is to study models of effectiveness. Therefore, before we share specific strategies with you, we describe a beginning teacher who modeled effective instructional leadership.

MEET MS. JONES: AN OUTSTANDING BEGINNING TEACHER

During the Fall 2012 semester, I (Gail) had the privilege of visiting the classroom of a beginning teacher, whom I will refer to as "Ms. Jones." This young White woman taught in a large public high school in the Midwest. I arrived at her classroom shortly before the students came in from lunch to a combined English and History class that she co-taught with another teacher.

When the bell rang, signaling that the lunch period had ended, Ms. Jones stood at the door and greeted each student. Once they entered the classroom, students saw that Ms. Jones had already written the homework assignment and agenda for the day on the whiteboard. By the time the tardy bell rang, approximately 40 students from racially diverse backgrounds were seated in numerous rows.

Ms. Jones officially began the class session by asking students to take out the required materials and end side conversations. Next, she read the information on the whiteboard orally. In addition to providing an overview of the day's agenda—to analyze documents to determine whether Hammurabi's Code was fair—she reviewed key points from the previous day's lesson plan. Next, after patiently answering several students' questions, Ms. Jones gave her class a five-minute time limit to summarize the previous day's assignment. Most students followed directions.

During the interactive lesson that followed, Ms. Jones shared information about Hammurabi's Code and showed students how to locate relevant information on the document they were analyzing. Throughout this process, she answered questions and asked questions that students were eager to answer. She also made sure that as many students as possible answered questions by frequently stating, "Some people whom I haven't seen raising hands, I'm going to be calling on you."

As I observed Ms. Jones and her class, I marveled at how well this young teacher was able to work effectively with such a large and racially diverse group of students. Although some students did engage in side conversations, and a few asked or answered questions so softly that it was difficult for me (and undoubtedly, their classmates) to hear them, I was impressed by what I had seen and left her classroom wishing that I'd had such a great history teacher during my high school years. Now, we'd like for you to share your thoughts about this story by completing the following exercise.

EXERCISE   What You Learned From Ms. Jones's Story (Part 1)

1. What are your overall thoughts about this story?

_____

_____

_____

_____

2. In your opinion, what are the main reasons why this young teacher worked effectively with such a large and racially diverse group of learners?

_____

_____

_____

_____

FACTORS THAT CONTRIBUTED TO MS. JONES'S SUCCESS AS AN INSTRUCTIONAL LEADER

Because I only observed Ms. Jones for one class period, I can only surmise why she was able to demonstrate outstanding instructional leadership during my visit. However, the following behaviors clearly contributed to her effectiveness:

Ms. Jones's Effective Instructional Leadership Qualities

1. She was prepared by already having the homework assignment and day's agenda on the whiteboard.

2. She used the relationship-building strategy of greeting students at the door.

3. As soon as the bell rang, she set the tone for learning by having students take out the needed materials and by asking them to refrain from talking to their classmates.

4. She used a recursive style of teaching by reviewing the previous day's lesson.

5. Throughout the class period, she kept the students interested and engaged by using diverse instructional practices: reviewing, mini-lectures, modeling, questioning, providing lots of examples, and allowing students to work independently and as a whole class.

6. She patiently answered all questions.

7. She used humor.

8. She made the subject matter relevant to students' daily lives by asking questions such as "Are there certain rules and laws, even in this building, with which we don't agree?"

9. Instead of standing in front of the classroom, she walked around the room.

10. She created an environment in which it was safe for students to make mistakes.

11. She often gave compliments, such as "Melissa, I like that, but I want to add a little context to it." "Thank you, Van. I forgot. That was a very important key point." "Very good question, Emily."

12. She modeled what she wanted students to do: "We're going to do 'A' together. Then, you're going to work in small groups."

13. She allowed students to leave the classroom in order to go to the restroom when necessary.

14. She didn't take herself too seriously and even mentioned a few of her imperfections.

15. She had decorated the classroom with important and relevant posters, famous quotes, studying tips, photos, and postcards.

16. Throughout the entire class session, she modeled respect by the manner in which she spoke to students, replied to their questions, encouraged them, and corrected them.

Now, please complete the following related exercise.

EXERCISE   What You Learned From Ms. Jones's Story (Part 2)

1. Which of the effective instructional leadership qualities or behaviors on the above list do you regularly practice or utilize?

_____

_____

_____

_____

2. Which of the effective instructional leadership qualities on the above list do you need to add to your repertoire of instructional strategies?

_____

_____

_____

_____

3. How can this story help you to work more effectively with students of color?

_____

_____

_____

_____

4. If you could interview Ms. Jones, what would you ask her?

_____

_____

_____

_____

EFFECTIVE TEACHING FROM ENGLISH LANGUAGE LEARNERS' PERSPECTIVES

In terms of becoming an outstanding instructional leader for all students, finding ways to meet the academic needs of students from racially and linguistically diverse backgrounds should be listed among your main goals. Of course, one of the best ways for you to strengthen your teaching skills is to learn from effective teachers, such as Ms. Jones. However, a second way is to learn from students of color. Because many teachers find it challenging to work with English language learners (ELLs), we believe that this is a topic that you need to know more about.

Although there is a lot of research about what works best for ELLs, much of it is based on the adult perspective. However, in the next section, you have an opportunity to learn from former ELL students themselves. Their feedback comes from a study that I (Gail) conducted, for which I collected narratives and questionnaire data from 69 tenth graders who had been non-English speakers or limited-English speakers during their early school years. I asked the students to identify the best and least effective strategies that their teachers used to help them learn to speak English and to offer advice to teachers. The six most frequently cited strategies involved using literature, oral practice, teaching the basics, offering individual help, allowing students to interact with their peers, and using games in the classroom.[6] The students' quotes below explain instructional strategies that you can use to help both ELLs and other students.

Using Literature

Comment 1:

> The teacher read books and other works to us that were appropriate for our age. Her system of teaching was that she read a word or line to us out loud and then we repeated [it]. Then she went on with paragraphs and we would remember the sound of the words when we saw them and were able to read out loud ourselves.[7]

Comment 2:

> When the teachers read to us in Spanish and then in English, or the other way around, pictures in books helped, as well as the dialogue.[8]

Oral Practice

Comment 3:

> I remember the teacher playing games with the class on how to pronounce each letter of the alphabet. She would give out small prizes to whomever pronounced a certain letter correctly and spelled a word with it. Eager, but too shy to participate, I paid close attention to the pronunciations and spelling of each letter and word during the game.

With the help of friends and classmates, I eventually learned how to pronounce each letter of the alphabet. After learning how to pronounce each letter properly, I went on to learn small words and grew from there.[9]

Teaching the Basics

Comment 4:

I started to learn the ABCs in English. That was the first thing I learned. After that, my teacher taught me the numbers 1–10. I personally believe that when you are teaching a child English, you should start with the ABCs, then the numbers, and start doing basic and common words that we usually use, and lastly, some sentences. After the child has learned this, you should start making small conversations and they'll try to answer. For me, this was very helpful, because you should always start with the easy stuff and end up with the hard stuff.[10]

Offering Individual Help

Comment 5:

When I was in first grade, I got help from a teacher's aide. She helped me learn how to read and write in English. She was very patient with me. First, she told me to sound out each letter and then put them together. That's how I learned to read.[11]

Comment 6:

I believe that some strategies could either help or shatter a student's confidence. The best strategy is to give them individual help outside the class.[12]

Allowing Students to Interact With Their Peers

Comment 7:

I had a tutor to help me, but I have to say that communicating with my friends was the most effective way that helped me to learn how to speak English.[13]

Comment 8:

It is much better to have all the students interact with each other. That way, the bilingual students will pick up English more rapidly and the English students might pick up something from another language.[14]

Comment 9:

> One day, while everyone else was working, my teacher called a young boy and me up to her desk. She told him something and then he glanced at me. All of a sudden, he asked me my name in Cambodian. I was so happy to know that there was someone else that spoke my language. So, I answered him back in Cambodian. Then, he told me that he was my partner in the class. In only a week, I memorized the alphabet.[15]

Using Games in the Classroom

Comment 10:

> I believe the best strategy to teach English to students who do not speak it is to make it fun. Although some students will not want to participate in a game to learn, they, like me, will learn little by little.[16]

Comment 11:

> The teacher would make games with Spanish and English words. One example of a game is they would put a pair of words in English and Spanish and then mix them up. We, the students, had to find the pairs of the English and Spanish words.[17]

INEFFECTIVE STRATEGIES FOR ELLS

The students also described the least effective strategies for ELLs. The following five were the most frequently cited.

Being Forced to Read in Front of the Class

Comment 12:

> I think it is a bad strategy to make them read aloud in front of other kids when they really can't. Teachers should give them time and make them more welcome by talking to them in Spanish first, and later in English. They shouldn't expect them right away to do everything in English.[18]

Being Corrected by Other Students and Being Segregated From Others

Comment 13:

> Something that did not help me at all was when my teachers would make me read in front of the class. This made me really self-conscious about the way I talked. I hated it when other students corrected me when I would say something wrong. It was embarrassing. Something

else that I know would not help is dividing the bilingual students from the English-speaking students. This, in my opinion, would cause division among peers and would most likely lead to conflict.[19]

Ignoring and Embarrassing ELLs

Comment 14:

> I believe that the one and only worst strategy that a teacher can have is to ignore and just give up on a student.[20]

Comment 15:

> One thing that would be really bad for the students is to dislike the English language . . . It all lies in the hands of the teacher, and how he or she presents it. No teacher should ever get frustrated with any student because I know how hard it is to go from one language to another.[21]

Comment 16:

> I had one bad experience when I was in second grade. The teacher would teach at a very fast pace. She would always pick me to do an exercise in front of the class and I still didn't know English very well. So, every time I said something wrong, she would embarrass me. From having this experience I would just like to tell teachers to get to know their students and teach at students' own pace, not theirs.[22]

Not Providing Adequate Assistance to ELLs

Comment 17:

> The best advice I could give to teachers who have students who don't speak English is to treat them like the students who do speak English. Don't neglect them. Be very patient with them.[23]

Covering Information Too Rapidly

Comment 18:

> My advice to teachers who have students who don't speak English is be patient with the students and guide them step by step. The best strategy for the students is pairing them with other students who speak the same language and English. Finally, don't expect the students to learn the language in a year or less. It takes a lot of time to convert one language to another.[24]

Now, please complete the following related exercise.

EXERCISE **Learning From the ELLs**

1. Which of the effective strategies for ELLs do you already use?

_____

_____

_____

_____

2. Which, if any, of the ineffective strategies for ELLs do you use?

_____

_____

_____

_____

3. Which comments from the students were the most informative to you?

_____

_____

_____

_____

4. What are the specific ways that you plan to use the students' comments to become a better instructional leader for students of color and ELLs?

_____

_____

_____

_____

CONCLUSION

In this chapter, we provided you with information from the TC Study, a beginning teacher, and former ELL students in order to help you to become an outstanding instructional leader of all students, but especially students of color. The following strategies and professional growth exercises are additional resources.

ADVICE AND STRATEGIES

1. Make sure your teaching methods are sound.

Make sure that the content of what you are teaching is based on research. Parents or community members who challenge you will have little basis for attacking you on a lesson gone bad if what you are teaching is based on research and proven practices.

During your teacher certification process, you undoubtedly became familiar with a lot of this research. In each chapter of this book, we have also recommended additional readings that will empower you. Throughout your teaching career, you will also have opportunities to attend professional development workshops and conferences that will allow you to remain current in terms of new research about effective instruction.

2. Make your job as easy as possible.

The Internet contains a wealth of information for educators. Research-based strategies, lesson plans, and worksheets are available for you to utilize. In addition to the U.S. Department of Education's website (as we suggested in an earlier chapter), you should also visit your state's department of education in order to find standards-based curricula for grade levels and subjects that you teach. We will return to the topic of standards-based lesson plans later in this chapter.

3. Modify your lesson plans to meet your students' academic needs.

As early in the school year as possible, find out if any of your students are ELLs or have learning disabilities. Modify your lesson plans accordingly.

4. Mentally practice.

As a former athlete, mental practice was a big part of my (Rufus's) life. This confidence-building strategy is an easy way to alleviate nervousness about teaching, especially if you are trying a new approach or teaching a subject or topic for the first time. The point is that you can practice in your head and visualize yourself delivering a lesson. Yes, it takes time, but it will make you a better teacher. During your mental practice exercises, you can anticipate how students might react and how you can respond.

5. Use different modalities.

Remember that one of the main reasons why Ms. Jones was able to work effectively with such a large and racially diverse group of students is that she used multiple teaching strategies during one class session. This is something that you should strive for. Questioning, quizzing, reviewing, and modeling are four ways that you can allow students to contribute to the lesson, and it also enables them to assume some of the responsibility for their learning.

Early on, identify the students who tune in when you are using certain strategies. You may have discipline issues from one student when he or she is writing but another student when he or she is reading. A specific type of assignment or exercise (writing, oral reading, etc.) may be the trigger. Learn from students' behaviors and find ways to diversify your lesson plans so that all students can be successful. For example, a student who strays off task during a writing assignment may work better when he or she is allowed to collaborate with another student on various writing assignments.

6. Teach lessons and give assignments on which students are likely to be successful.

Teaching lessons on which students are likely to be successful is a great confidence booster before you move to more difficult material. The positive feeling that you get from watching your students being successful will make you feel better about yourself, and the students may feel better about you and themselves. Building their confidence is one of the best ways to strengthen your relations with students and build student morale, especially for students who have historically underachieved.

7. Talk less; empower students more.

Giving students brief instructions; mini-lessons; letting them work in small groups; and having them work at stations, learning centers, or pods can be mutually beneficial to you and your students. For you, it will require less talking and decrease the likelihood that discipline problems stemming from boredom will occur. It will also give you opportunities to provide individualized or small-group instruction to struggling students. Students benefit by having opportunities to interact with their peers, and being in a classroom in which multiple activities occur is very likely to be more interesting than sitting in one where the teacher gives lengthy lectures and then expects students to work in silence for the duration of the class session.

8. Keep hope alive.

One of the most frustrating aspects of teaching is that often it takes time—sometimes a long time—to see the results of one's hard work. As a teacher, when you do your very best to provide students with lessons that are based on outstanding instructional practices, and they fail a quiz, underperform on a standardized test, continue to read below grade level, or fail to understand a fundamental math concept, it can become easy to feel like a failure or to blame the students or their parents. During such times, it's important to realize that for students who have historically underachieved, struggled with a subject, or entered your class with skills that were far below grade level, the tests that are used may not measure the progress that they actually made as a result of your teaching. Therefore, you have to find ways to keep encouraging yourself, to keep working hard, and to continue to believe that your students—even struggling students, low-income students, and students from historically underserved backgrounds—can succeed academically.

A good way to do this is to keep a log or record in your journal of every positive experience—no matter how small—that you have with your students. If a student couldn't orally decode a sentence at the beginning of the school term but begins to decode words more fluently, record it. If a student who could not add or subtract positive or negative numbers accurately learns to do so, record it. Reviewing these signs of progress periodically can inspire you when circumstances look bleak.

9. Know how to create culturally relevant standards-based lesson plans.

Many states have already adopted new standards that are based on the Common Core State Standards Initiative.

> The Common Core State Standards (CCSS) are a set of high quality academic expectations in English-language arts (ELA) and mathematics that define the knowledge and skills all students should master by the end of each grade level in order to be on track for success in college and career.[25]

In addition to knowing the standards that you are required to address for the subjects and grade level(s) that you teach, it is also important that you find ways to create culturally relevant standards-based lesson plans. Therefore, we have included the following three-day lesson plans to make it easier for you to understand how to do this. The first three-day lesson plan was developed by our daughter, NaChe' Thompson, who is an outstanding beginning teacher. The second three-day lesson plan is one that I (Gail) used when I taught high school. However, it can be adapted for upper-elementary schools students (fourth and fifth graders) and middle school students. The different formats that were used will give you an idea of options that you can consider as you design your own lesson plans. Of course, you are also welcome to use the lesson plans that we provided and modify them to suit your needs.

A Three-Day Culturally Relevant Standards-Based Lesson Plan

by NaChe' L. Thompson, High School English Teacher

Grade Level: 12

Lesson Title: Desiree's Baby

Standard: Analyze recognized works of world literature from a variety of authors.

Objective: Students will analyze recognized works of literature from a variety of authors during Short Story Boot Camp. ("Desiree's Baby" by Kate Chopin)

(Continued)

(Continued)

Day 1

Warm Up:"Virginian Luxuries"

Students will analyze the painting "Virginian Luxuries." Students will respond on paper to the following: "What message does the artist convey?" Students will share their analyses. (15 minutes)

Anticipatory Set: Imitation of Life

Teacher will explain that one of the central causes of conflict in "Desiree's Baby" is the idea of "passing for White." Teacher will introduce this concept by playing a scene from the film *Imitation of Life*. (12-minute clip)

　　Teacher will ask students to work in teams to discuss the film clip with a classmate. (5 minutes)

　　Teacher will call the class back together to share the content of their teams' discussion. Teacher will add anything left out. (3–5 minutes)

Direct Instruction: Historical Context of "Desiree's Baby"

Teacher will use the "Historical Context of 'Desiree's Baby'" PowerPoint slides as an aid in the explanation of the historical context of the story. Teacher will take notes. (15 minutes)

Closure: Teacher will remind students to read Perrine's Chapter 2, pages 103–110 and answer #1–6 on page 111. (Insert a due date.)

Day 2

English:"Desiree's Baby"

Standard: Analyze recognized works of world literature from a variety of authors.

Objective: Students will analyze recognized works of literature from a variety of authors during Short Story Boot Camp. ("Desiree's Baby" by Kate Chopin)

Warm Up: Students will complete the written warm-up, which asks them to reflect on the scene from *Imitation of Life*. (5 minutes)

Anticipatory Set: Students will share their responses with the class. (3–5 minutes)

Direct Instruction: Teams will work together to read "Desiree's Baby" aloud. (10–15 minutes)

Guided Practice: Teacher will give students time to review the story and extract the story's elements with their teams. (15 minutes) Teacher will take notes as teams map the story on the board.

Independent Practice: Students will begin their short fiction data page.

Homework: Short Fiction Data Page

Day 3

English:"Desiree's Baby"

Standard: Analyze recognized works of world literature from a variety of authors.

Objective: Students will analyze recognized works of literature from a variety of authors during Short Story Boot Camp. ("Desiree's Baby" by Kate Chopin)

Warm Up: Students will take out their short fiction data pages (homework). Teacher will check homework, read a newspaper or magazine article about the heritage of Michelle Obama, and contrast the ideas in the article with those of "Desiree's Baby." (15 minutes)

Anticipatory Set: Teacher will review the homework. Teacher will ask students to share any ambiguities or irony they found in the story. (10 minutes)

Direct Instruction: Teacher will post the timed writing prompt and read it to students.

Guided Practice: Teacher will ask students to sift through the prompt to identify their task.

Independent Practice: Students will complete a timed writing, which requires them to infer the cultural and moral values of the story's society, based on the alienation of Desiree and her baby.

Closure: Teacher will collect the timed writing and ask students to identify the easiest and most challenging aspects of the task.

A Three-Day Culturally Relevant Standards-Based Lesson Plan

The Time Line Project

Note: Although it can be done at any time, this project is a great first-week-of-school activity that can help you get to know your students better and learn important information about their reading and writing skills and their willingness and ability to follow directions. It is also a great relationship-building project.

Grade Level: 6

Subject: Language Arts

Topic: Time Line Project

Time Span: 3 days

Materials Needed: Art supplies such as construction paper, colored markers, crayons, butcher paper, pencils, and glue sticks

Related Standards:

- **ELA.6.SL.1** Engage effectively in a range of collaborative discussions (one-on-one, in groups, and teacher-led) with diverse partners on Grade 6 topics, texts, and issues, building on others' ideas and expressing their own clearly.

(Continued)

(Continued)

- **ELA.6.SL.4** Present claims and findings, sequencing ideas logically and using pertinent descriptions, facts, and details to accentuate main ideas or themes; use appropriate eye contact, adequate volume, and clear pronunciation.

- **ELA.6.W.4** Produce clear and coherent writing in which the development, organization, and style are appropriate to task, purpose, and audience. (Grade-specific expectations for writing types are defined in standards 1–3 above.)

- **ELA.6.W.10** Write routinely over extended time frames (time for research, reflection, and revision) and shorter time frames (a single sitting or a day or two) for a range of discipline-specific tasks, purposes, and audiences.

Objective: Using their personalized time lines as a prewriting activity, students will write a related paragraph and share it orally with the class. These activities will allow the teacher to assess students' basic writing skills and oral reading skills.

Teacher Preparation:

1. Following the guidelines below for students, create your own colorful, personalized time line, and then write a paragraph (see the details below) about one significant event that occurred in your life.

2. Show your time line to your students.

3. Read your paragraph to your students.

4. Explain that students are going to also create their own time lines, write a related paragraph, and share the paragraph with the class.

Day 1: Creating the Time Line

Structure: Small Group Activity

Purpose: To develop a colorful, personalized time line

Guidelines:

1. After you share your time line with the class, explain that they will create their own colorful, personalized time lines that will be graded and used to decorate the classroom walls.

2. Explain that students can design their time lines in any way they choose. However, they must:
   a. list the 10 most important events of their life on the time line, including at least three that pertain to some aspect of their racial or cultural heritage,
   b. include the year and their age when each event occurred on the time line,
   c. include a drawing or symbol to represent each event, and
   d. write their name on the time line.

3. Ask if there are any questions, and if so, answer them.

4. Divide students into groups of four or five. Ask one student from each group to get art supplies for each group member.

5. Advise students to write the 10 events and corresponding years in pencil first and then decorate their time lines.

6. Approximately 10 minutes before the class period ends, ask one student per group to return the art supplies to the designated place in the classroom.

Homework: Ask students to finish their time lines and to proofread them carefully. Students who need to borrow art supplies may return after school to do so.

Ask students to select one event on their time lines as the basis for the paragraph that they will write on the following day.

Assessment:

Keeping in mind that one of the purposes of this project is to create a community of learners through relationship building, the following grading scale can be used to evaluate students' time lines.

A = Superior (exceeds requirements)

B = Good (met basic requirements)

C = Fair (did not meet all basic requirements)

After the time lines have been graded, post all of them in your classroom.

Day 2: Writing a Basic Paragraph

Structure: Students will work independently.

Purpose: Students will demonstrate that they can write a basic paragraph that is based on a historical, racial, or cultural event in their lives and that they can follow directions.

Guidelines:

1. Review yesterday's in-class and homework assignment.

2. Give an overview of today's lesson.

3. Read your own personal paragraph to the class.

4. Tell students that they will select one event from their time lines as the basis for their own paragraphs, which they will be sharing with the class on the following day.

5. Inform students that their paragraphs:
   a. must be neat and legible when they hand it in the following day,
   b. must contain a title that is centered at the top of the page,
   c. must contain a topic sentence,
   d. must contain three to five supporting details,
   e. must contain a closing statement,
   f. should not contain spelling errors, and

(Continued)

(Continued)

  g. should not contain fragments or incomplete sentences;

  h. Each sentence should begin with a capital letter and end with the proper punctuation mark.

6. Advise students to spend some time outlining their paragraphs before they begin to write it.

7. Ask if there are any questions.

8. Ask students to work on their paragraphs quietly and independently but inform them that they may raise their hands or come over to your desk if they have questions.

9. Allow students to work on their paragraphs for the remainder of the class session except for the last 10 minutes.

10. During the last 10 minutes of the class session, answer questions, explain the homework assignment, provide an overview of the next day, and collect the time lines.

Homework: Students will revise, rewrite, and proofread their paragraphs several times.

Assessment:

After you have collected the paragraphs, consider using the following grading scale:

  A = Superior (exceeds requirements)
  B = Good (met basic requirements, but may contain one error)
  C = Satisfactory (did not meet all basic requirements or contains one or two errors)
  D = Needs to Improve (did not meet all basic requirements and contains several errors)

Day 3: Sharing the Autobiographical Paragraph

Structure: Whole-Class Activity

Purpose: to read an autobiographical paragraph to the entire class

Guidelines:

1. Review yesterday's in-class assignment and the homework assignment.

2. Provide an overview of today's objective: to share the autobiographical paragraph with the class

3. Inform students that they will be reading their paragraphs orally to the entire class.

4. Explain that everyone should listen quietly as others are reading, be respectful by treating their classmates as they want to be treated, and applaud after each paragraph is read.

5. Ask students to volunteer to read their paragraphs. (If no one volunteers to do so immediately, offer extra credit to the first three students who

volunteer to read their paragraphs.) Then tell students that you will call on them to read in alphabetical order according to their last names.

6. As each student is reading, take notes:
   a. Did the student read fluently?
   b. Did the student write about a traumatic event of which I need to be aware?
   c. Does the paragraph make sense?
   d. Did the student follow directions?
   e. Did the student share information that may help me to understand his or her culture better?

7. As soon as each student finishes reading his or her paragraph, start applauding, and after the applause has ended, give the student some type of compliment:

   "That was a very interesting paragraph."

   "Great job."

   "Your paragraph is very informative."

   "I learned something new from your paragraph."

   "That was awesome."

   "You have the potential to become a good author."

   "I loved your opening sentence."

   "That was a creative closing sentence."

   "Your paragraph is organized well."

8. Collect each paragraph.

9. Tell students that after the paragraphs have been graded, they will have an opportunity to revise their paragraphs for a higher grade.

10. Use the feedback that you learn from their paragraphs to determine if you need to develop remedial writing lessons regarding how to write basic sentences and basic paragraphs or whether or not your students are ready to do more advanced types of writing.

Homework: Ask students to write another basic paragraph (using the guidelines for Day 2) to explain what they thought of the three-day Time Line Project: what they liked, what they disliked, what they learned, and so on.

Assessment:

Note: Because of the current emphasis on positive behavior supports and relationship-building, some school leaders discourage teachers from giving failing grades to students. Therefore, please modify the following grading scale to suit your beliefs, values, professional obligations, and school/district expectations.

Consider giving an "A" to each student who read his or her paragraph orally and an "F" or "I" to any student who refused to do so.

Source: Adapted from *Through Ebony Eyes: What Teachers Need to Know but Are Afraid to Ask About African American Students.*[26]

APPLYING WHAT YOU LEARNED TO YOUR *YES, I CAN!* JOURNAL

1. Visit the U.S. Department of Education website. Make a list of and print resources for your grade level and subject areas that you can use in your lesson plans.
2. Find three culturally relevant video clips on the Internet that you can use to supplement three of your lesson plans.
3. Design five culturally relevant standards-based lesson plans for your students.
4. Ask colleagues to share culturally relevant standards-based lesson plans that they have designed with you.
5. Ask your department chair or a school leader to designate a professional development time for you and other teachers to collaborate on developing culturally relevant standards-based lesson plans.
6. Read the following quote from a former ELL student who participated in a study that I (Gail) conducted.

   When I entered kindergarten in East Los Angeles, I couldn't speak English or read or write. I was isolated from the rest of the class. I felt neglected by my teacher and my classmates. They would try to communicate with me but it was no use. Tears would roll down from my eyes.[27]

   In your journal, explain what you would do to help this student thrive in your classroom.

7. View the film clip from Nicole Franklin's documentary (www.Little BrotherFilm.com), and summarize your thoughts, reactions, and ways that you can use this information to become a better teacher.
8. Read the following works and, in your journal, summarize your thoughts, reactions, and ways that you can use this information.
   - *Teach With Your Heart: Lessons I Learned From the Freedom Writers* by Erin Gruwell
   - *Deciding What to Teach & Test: Developing, Aligning, and Leading the Curriculum* by Fenwick English
   - *There Are No Shortcuts: How an Inner-City Teacher—Winner of the American Teacher Award—Inspires His Students and Challenges Us to Rethink the Way We Educate Our Children* by Rafe Esquith

Can't We All Just Get Along? 6

Using the Curriculum to Improve Race Relations in Class

MEET CHAU: AN ASIAN AMERICAN STUDENT (PART 1)

Chau immigrated to the United States from Vietnam. Because her parents had very limited English skills, when her mother enrolled Chau in kindergarten, her mother had trouble communicating with the teacher. However, as a concerned parent, she did her best to inform the teacher that Chau's name was pronounced "Jo." After her mother left the classroom, Chau thought that she would enjoy school, but one incident changed her opinion. She explained,

> After that, all the mothers went home, and I along with the other kids, listened to our teacher read a book. I liked her. The next day, she assigned seats. She said "Chau, you sit here." I looked at her but I did not say anything. The fat little boy who sat in front of me, laughed and said, "Your name is Chau?" A horrible feeling suddenly crept into my stomach.[1]

EXERCISE Now It's Your Turn (Part 1)

By now, you know that during your teaching career, numerous students from racially diverse backgrounds will probably be assigned to your classroom. You also know that you can use these opportunities to improve students' lives and increase their chances of having a bright future. So we'd like for you to pretend that Chau is one of your students and answer the following questions:

1. In your opinion, what caused the horrible feeling to suddenly creep into Chau's stomach?

_____

_____

_____

_____

2. In your opinion, why did Chau refuse to respond when the teacher told her where to sit?

_____

_____

_____

_____

3. If Chau were one of your students, what specific strategies would you use to help her succeed in your classroom?

_____

_____

_____

_____

4. Based on the limited information that we shared with you about Chau, how do you think she turned out as an adult?

_____

_____

_____

_____

MEET CHAU: AN ASIAN AMERICAN STUDENT (PART 2)

Reading the second part of Chau's story in her own words will help you understand why the "horrible feeling suddenly crept into [her] stomach" and why things went downhill for her, starting on the second day of school.

From then on, the teacher always pronounced my name "Chau," like "Puppy Chow," and that fat little boy always had something to say. I tried to correct her once but she could not understand what I was trying to say. I began to accept it.

To this day, I regret not correcting her. In my own way, I blame her for all of the torment I endured throughout elementary school because of my name. My name, as well as my limited English, would keep me different from all those other kids. Until I got older, "Chau" would remain the one word I hated most.[2]

Because of her early negative experiences at school, Chau could easily have become another casualty. Her parents did not speak English well, and she could not even communicate with or understand her kindergarten teacher. On top of all of this, another student was allowed to bully her. Instead of becoming an underachiever who eventually dropped out of school, Chau defied the odds. She worked hard, learned English, became the salutatorian of her high school, and went to college.

EXERCISE   Now It's Your Turn (Part 2)

1. Now that you have read both parts of the story, what can you learn from it that can help you to work more effectively with students of color and English language learners (ELLs)?

_____

_____

_____

_____

2. If you were Chau's kindergarten teacher, what would you have done differently than her actual teacher did?

_____

_____

_____

_____

CHAPTER HIGHLIGHTS

We hope that Chau's story helped you to realize how easy it is for teachers to unknowingly worsen a child's schooling experiences by engaging in or allowing subtle or even blatant acts of cultural insensitivity to occur in the classroom. Chau's teacher did this when she failed to (1) learn how to pronounce Chau's name correctly, (2) stop the other student from making fun of Chau's name, and (3) make more of an effort to communicate with Chau and understand what Chau was trying to tell her.

By now, you know that our main goal is to help you to become an outstanding instructional leader of all students, especially African American students and other students of color. You also know that outstanding instructional leadership requires strong classroom management skills and the ability to prepare and deliver comprehensible lessons to students of color, ELLs, and struggling students. Of course, it also requires that you possess the correct mindset about your ability to work effectively with students of color. In this chapter, we return to the mindset work by focusing specifically on issues pertaining to cultural insensitivity in the classroom. In addition to sharing what the Teacher Confidence (TC) Study respondents said, we'll ask you to rate yourself and compare and contrast your beliefs with those of the TC Study respondents, and we will present basic information about cultural insensitivity and strategies that can help you address and prevent cultural conflicts from arising in your classroom.

Basic Facts About Cultural Insensitivity and Racism

Cultural insensitivity constitutes seemingly lesser offensive comments or acts that tend to stem from stereotypes and ignorance about individuals or groups from cultural backgrounds that are different from one's own. Racism encompasses race-based discrimination or negative differential behavior that is designed to keep groups and individuals in inferior positions solely because of their racial background. Nevertheless, it is often difficult to differentiate between racism and cultural insensitivity. Therefore, the following list, which was compiled from the book, *Exploring the Culture of Arrogance in the Academy: A Blueprint for Increasing Black Faculty Satisfaction,* (which I [Gail] wrote with Dr. Angela Louque) and also from my (Gail's) book, *The Power of One: How You Can Help or Harm African American Students,* should be helpful.

1. "Although cultural insensitivity may stem from ignorance and innocence, and may be less overt, and appear to be less offensive and seemingly less harmful than racist acts, its effects cannot be underestimated."[3]

2. Both racism and cultural insensitivity can be either overt or subtle.[4]

3. Racism and cultural insensitivity are common in Pre-K–12 schools and in higher education, but they usually manifest themselves in subtle ways.[5]

4. Instructional leaders are responsible for ensuring that all students are able to receive a quality education in a safe learning environment.[6]

5. "[M]any educators are just as uncomfortable as most other Americans when it comes to having honest and forthright conversations about race."[7]

6. Many teachers "don't even feel comfortable discussing racial issues in their classrooms."[8]

EXERCISE **Examining Your Teaching Self-Confidence About Racial Problems and Cultural Conflicts**

1. Have you ever been subjected to cultural insensitivity? If so, what happened and how did it affect you?

_____

_____

_____

_____

2. Have you ever been subjected to racism? If so, what happened and how did it affect you?

_____

_____

_____

_____

3. How confident are you about your ability to incorporate racial issues into your lesson plans and why?

_____

_____

_____

_____

4. How confident are you about your ability to effectively address racial conflicts that may arise in your classroom and why?

_____

_____

_____

_____

5. Please review your answers and summarize what you can learn from them.

_____

_____

_____

_____

WHY KNOWING HOW TO HANDLE RACIAL CONFLICTS THAT MAY ARISE IN YOUR CLASSROOM AND INCORPORATING RACIAL ISSUES INTO YOUR LESSON PLANS ARE IMPORTANT

One of the messages that we have repeatedly conveyed to you is that many teachers have good intentions yet fail woefully with certain students, especially African American students and other students of color, students from low-income backgrounds, and struggling students. A primary cause is unaddressed mindsets that are rooted in stereotypes, fear, and even racist beliefs. These unaddressed issues can cause teachers to unknowingly subject students to negative differential treatment through their instructional practices and discipline policies and practices. Consequently, students may become resentful, for even if teachers are in denial or unaware that their biases are noticeable, students notice them. The following quotes from students who participated in one of the studies that I (Gail) conducted for my book, *Up Where We Belong: Helping African American and Latino Students Rise in School and in Life*, illustrate this point.

According to a Latina high school student,

I'm Hispanic, and if it's a group of my Hispanic friends, and we're sitting in back, talking whatever, and there's a couple of [W]hite girls in the front talking, the teacher will yell at us and tell us to shut up. But the two girls up in the front don't get told anything.[9]

An African American female at the same school, remarked,

There's one particular English teacher . . . and it's only because I am the only [B]lack student in that class. So, she picks on me at a constant pace: "Oh, you're talking. Well, I saw *you.*" I'm like, "But she's talking to me. I'm commenting on what she said." The teacher says, "Well, I saw *you* talking, so you're going to get the disciplinary action." If I don't back off, she's going to yell at me and pinpoint me, but I haven't done anything wrong.[10]

When teachers fail to face and address their biases, students may lose respect for the teacher, accuse the teacher of being racist, become apathetic, misbehave, spread negative rumors about the teacher, or (in rare cases) act out physically. For example, when I (Gail) was a high school teacher, another teacher was assaulted by a student who accused the teacher of being racist against Latinos. In another case, an African American elementary school student refused to take the standardized test because he believed that his teacher was racist and would use his test scores to harm him. When the school principal told the child that he needed to take the test, the boy stated, "I ain't giving that [W]hite woman one more reason to say I'm dumb."[11]

In addition to resenting their teachers, students who believe that their teachers are racist or that the teachers have subjected them to negative differential treatment may begin to resent other students. For example, at the school where I (Gail) conducted the *Up Where We Belong* studies, racial conflicts were common among students. White students, especially females, said that they believed that African American male students harassed them, and fights between African American and Latino students often occurred. Furthermore, several African American and Latino students said that they did not like the preferential treatment that teachers gave to White students. This type of resentment can lead to classroom disruptions, such as verbal arguments and even fistfights among students. Therefore, in order to decrease the likelihood that your classroom will become a racially tense and potentially volatile setting, you must do all that you can to prevent this from happening. What's more, if a racial conflict happens to occur in your classroom, you need to know how to handle it. At the end of this chapter, we share several related strategies. However, the best strategy is to be preventative.

One of the best ways to decrease the likelihood that racial conflicts will erupt in your classroom is to take precautionary steps. This means that we urge you to do the mindset and professional growth work that we have recommended in every chapter. In other words, you will work hard to become the outstanding instructional leader that all students (especially African American students and other students of color, struggling students, and ELLs) deserve by creating a classroom climate that is based on fair and effective discipline practices. Additionally, you will provide them with an empowering curriculum. More specifically, when you design culturally rich and relevant lesson plans, you can offset potential racial conflicts from occurring among students.

Research has repeatedly shown that many students of color want a culturally relevant curriculum, such as the lesson plans that we included in the previous chapter. For example, 60 percent of the Latino students and 75 percent of the African American students who participated in the *Up Where We Belong* studies said they wanted to learn more about their culture in class.[12] A Latina student asked a pertinent question: "I've already learned a lot of American history my whole life, because I've lived here my whole life. So, it would be nice to learn something about my culture too. It wouldn't hurt, right?"[13] Similarly, an African American male student asked, "Where's the Mexican people in the history books? You don't be learning nothing about them."[14]

When the curriculum is interesting, comprehensible, and culturally relevant, both teachers and students benefit. Students of color are less likely to be bored in class and are more likely to be interested and engaged. Therefore, they will be less inclined to misbehave in class. They are also more likely to be motivated to excel academically. As one African American male participant in the *Up Where We Belong* studies explained, "I have AP History, and I find myself doing better on tests when I'm reading and writing about stuff that pertains to my culture. If they incorporated more of that, then maybe I could do better in that class."[15] In addition to having fewer discipline problems, preparing culturally relevant lessons will allow you to learn more about your students' backgrounds.

Hopefully, you now understand why it's important to be able to handle racial conflicts that may arise in your classroom, and you realize that you can decrease the chances of this happening by being proactive. Next, we'd like for you to examine Figure 6.1, read what the TC Study respondents said and then compare and contrast their answers with your beliefs.

Figure 6.1 How the TC Study Participants Rated Their Ability to Incorporate Racial Issues Into Their Lesson Plans and Their Ability to Handle Racial Conflicts That Arise in the Classroom

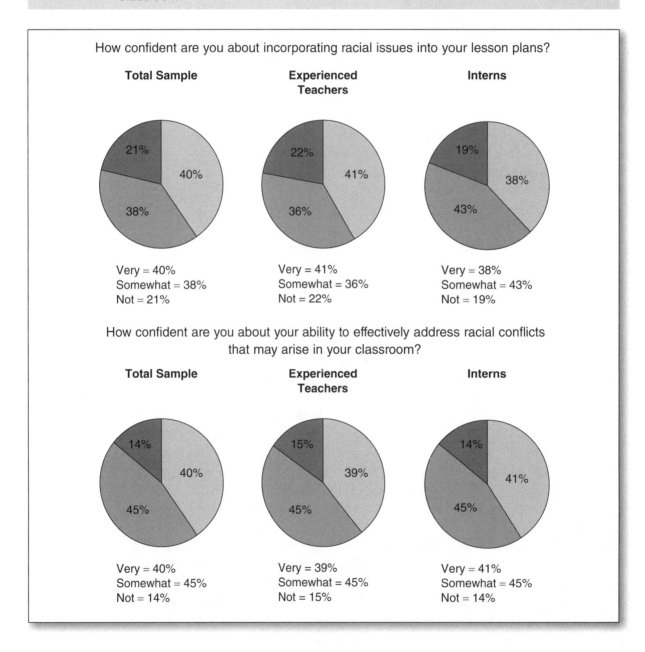

With the exception of working with parents who do not speak English, and working with struggling students, this was the area where the participants were least likely to feel confident. Regarding incorporating racial

issues into the curriculum, a White female middle school teacher with more than five years of teaching experience stated, "I could use some ideas on how to incorporate racial issues into my lesson plans." In explaining why she was only somewhat confident, a White intern explained,

> I know that people are different and that there are many different races and cultures in each classroom. So, I'm only somewhat confident about incorporating racial issues into my lesson plans, because I want to make sure they are engaging and relevant to all. With regard to racial conflicts, there is no colorblindness, and when it comes to that type of conflict, people need to know that they are different and that different is okay.

An Asian American male intern who had taught high school for one year was one of the few TC Study respondents who wrote about being very confident about his ability to address race-related issues. He stated,

> I am very confident in my teaching skills. I'm also very confident in my ability to work well with people. I do not tolerate racism. But I do like to talk about racism when it comes to knowing about a culture.

In terms of handling racial conflicts that arise in the classroom, a White teacher said, "I feel a little apprehensive about talking about racial conflict issues." A White female intern who had taught middle school math for one year said, "I am fairly confident in all the areas of teaching, and the only problem would be if there are conflicts that are racial. But I would handle them okay, I believe." Another intern, a White female with no teaching experience but who had worked as an instructional aide for several years, admitted, "I'm not very confident in any of these areas, but I still think this has to do with the fact that I've never had my own classroom. I'm timid about addressing racial conflicts, but also lack experience."

EXERCISE What You Learned From the TC Study Respondents

1. What are the most important points that you learned from the TC Study results and the respondents' answers?

_____

_____

_____

_____

(Continued)

(Continued)

2. Which comments differ from your views and why?

_____

_____

_____

_____

3. Which comments are most similar to your views and why?

_____

_____

_____

_____

CONCLUSION

What We Can Learn From the TC Study

In this chapter, we emphasized several points that we want you to remember:

- A culturally relevant curriculum is important.
- Many students of color want to learn more about their culture in class.
- A culturally relevant curriculum can benefit both teachers and students.
- A culturally relevant curriculum can decrease the likelihood that racial conflicts will arise in the classroom.

Nevertheless, the TC Study results clearly show that many teachers lack confidence about two related issues. Specifically,

- only 40 percent of the TC Study respondents were very confident about their ability to incorporate racial issues into their lesson plans; and
- only 40 percent of the respondents were very confident about their ability to effectively address racial conflicts that may arise in their classroom.

The following advice and strategies can help you increase your confidence about these matters.

ADVICE AND STRATEGIES

1. Tie the curriculum to standards.

In the previous chapter, we emphasized that because of the current high-stakes testing era, every lesson plan that you design should be based on one or more grade-level standards. Many of the materials that experts have already developed are standards based. Therefore, it is important that you utilize these materials to your advantage. For example, Gary Holland, an education consultant, has created culturally relevant curricula that have been used in many schools. According to the *Indianapolis Recorder*, "The Historic Journey curriculum is a comprehensive K–12 interdisciplinary curriculum that is aligned to Common Core State Standards. The curriculum, both text and web based, explores the literary, historical, social, scientific, mathematic and cultural endeavors of African Americans."[16] To learn more about Holland's work or to access teachers' guides, worksheets, and other materials, visit www.thehistoricjourney.org. Below, we share other examples that pertain to ELL students, Latinos, and Asian Americans.

2. Use students as a resource.

Asking students to complete culturally relevant assignments is one of the best ways to increase their interest and to empower them. For example, when I (Gail) taught high school, I assigned the Community Problem Solving Project, the All About Me Project, the Cultural Awareness Project, and the Time Line Project. Each assignment required students to write about topics that were relevant to their personal life, culture, and community and was designed to improve their reading, writing, speaking, and listening skills. Each of these assignments is explained in detail in the Appendix section of *Through Ebony Eyes: What Teachers Need to Know but Are Afraid to Ask About African American Students*.[17] You can also ask students, parents, and other educators for additional suggestions.

3. Use existing materials.

As we stated previously, it's important to remember that there is absolutely no need for you to start from scratch. Educational organizations, state departments of education, and the U.S. Department of Education websites contain culturally relevant lesson plans and other teaching materials. One document, "*A Report of Spanish Resources for Mathematics Teachers of English Language Learners*, contains a plethora of information for teachers who desire to use culturally relevant mathematics strategies. Lesson plans, games, math links for teachers, dictionaries, research reports, and diagnostic tests are among the materials that the authors of this report created for educators.[18]

One of the best places to locate a lot of culturally relevant information and materials that you can incorporate into your lesson plans is the Smithsonian Institute. To find historical information, teaching resources, art, museums, and lesson plans, visit the websites for the Smithsonian's American Indian Museum, African American History and Culture Museum, Anacostia Community Museum, African Art Museum, Asian Pacific Heritage Center, Latino Center, and Center for Folklife and Cultural Heritage. Knowing about and honoring each of the Heritage Month Celebrations instead of only commemorating Black History Month can decrease the likelihood that students will complain that one group is receiving preferential treatment and thereby prevent racial conflicts from flaring up.

4. Use current events.

Creating lessons plans that are based on current events is another easy way to make the curriculum culturally relevant and to also decrease the chances that racial conflicts will erupt in your classroom. Media reports often focus on racial issues. For example, in 2013, the George Zimmerman trial and the Paula Deen controversy dominated news stories for several months. The Zimmerman trial centered on whether or not a biracial (half-White, half-Latino) man had killed an African American teen in self-defense. The Paula Deen story centered around the issue of whether or not a famous White chef and restaurant owner was an antiblack racist. Assigning relevant reading assignments from magazines and newspapers, sharing related video clips, and allowing students to share their thoughts about these and other current events through class discussions, debates, and writing assignments will enable them to learn how to address controversial issues in a safe learning environment.

5. Create a culturally safe classroom environment.

Becoming an outstanding teacher of all students, especially students of color, requires that you create a culturally safe classroom environment. It's best to begin on the first day of school when you explain your class rules to students. Emphasizing that no name calling, bullying, or sexually or racially offensive language will be tolerated and holding offenders accountable are necessary. Furthermore, it's important that you set boundaries during class discussions by explaining to students how to voice their dissenting viewpoints in a respectful manner.

6. Address a common stereotype as early as possible.

Just as educators have historically misunderstood and misjudged certain students (especially African American, Latino, ELL, and low-income students), students often misjudge teachers. Educators arrive at school with unaddressed racial baggage about students, and students arrive at school with stereotypes about their classmates and about teachers. Some students may automatically assume that you are racist, and many teachers have been accused of being racist.

Instead of bursting into tears, becoming defensive, or retaliating against the accuser, we advise you to take steps to offset potential misunderstandings as early in the school year as possible.

One way to do this is to educate students about your culture. This means that you must first know and understand your own cultural history, which many teachers don't know or understand. Therefore, you will have to do your homework. Once you have done this, spend time sharing photos and artifacts about your ancestry, your upbringing, why you became a teacher, and so on with students. Afterward, ask them to do a similar project about their own heritage and allow them to share the finished product with the entire class. This is a great way to humanize yourself to your students and to also create a community of learners.

7. Use conflicts as teachable-moment opportunities.

No matter how hard you try to avoid cultural conflicts and no matter how hard you try to be fair and not to be misunderstood, misjudged, or mislabeled by students, reality and the law of probability suggest that racial conflicts may erupt in your classroom and also that you may be accused of being racist. If and when these events occur, remember the following:

- As the instructional leader, you are responsible for handling conflicts wisely and fairly.
- Examine what happened, try to figure out why it occurred, identify the lessons that you and your students can learn from the incident, and try to determine how you can prevent similar problems from recurring.
- Spend time discussing the incident with students and use questioning to uncover their thoughts about the causes, solutions, and lessons to be learned from the problem.
- Try to incorporate conflict-resolution stories, strategies, and assignments into your lesson plans.

8. Learn from the courageous preschool director.

In *Exposing the Culture of Arrogance in the Academy: A Blueprint for Increasing Black Faculty Satisfaction*, Dr. Angela Louque and I (Gail) shared a story about a White preschool director who handled a brewing racial conflict adeptly. At the school, the White children had gradually started to exclude the two African American preschoolers from their games, refused to hold their hands during a class activity where handholding was required, and had begun to make racially offensive remarks. Instead of ignoring the situation, minimizing it, or blaming the African American children, the director summoned all of the parents to an emergency meeting. During the meeting, she

> informed them of what had been happening, said the racist behavior was unacceptable, and discussed an action plan with them. One of the components of this action plan was that the curriculum would become more multicultural, in order to teach the children to value and appreciate other groups. The director was also holding the parents accountable for doing their part to ensure that the racist behavior would cease. Her actions sent a clear message to students, teachers, and parents that racism would not be tolerated at the school. This message was, undoubtedly, validating and reassuring to the [B]lack children and their parents.[19]

APPLYING WHAT YOU LEARNED TO YOUR *YES, I CAN!* JOURNAL

1. Read the following case study, which a parent shared with me (Gail).

During the 2009–2010 school year, 10-year-old April, an African American fifth grader, attended a high-performing southern California public elementary school. April loved school and earned five *A*s and four *B*s on her final report card. She was inquisitive, eager to learn, self-confident, and outgoing, and she also earned high citizenship marks.

In her spare time, April enjoyed reading books, and she and her mom often went to the public library to check out books. Because of her natural acting ability, April was also interested in taking acting classes. On Sundays, she attended Sunday School and church and served as a junior usher at her church.

The following summer, April and her mom moved to Phoenix, Arizona, and at the end of August, April entered sixth grade. April and an African American boy were the only African American children in their class. At the end of the first week of school, April's mother telephoned me to say that April had stood up to a group of White children who had tried to bully her in the lunchroom. April had also complained to her mother that the schoolwork, especially the math, was much easier than the work that she had done in fifth grade. Furthermore, April's mother told me that on two occasions that week, April's teacher had made questionable comments to her daughter.

In October 2010, April's mother became so fed up with the way that the teacher was treating her daughter that she transferred April to another school. At the new school, April was the only African American child in her classroom. Once again, she found that the schoolwork was way too easy for her. According to April's mother, within a month, April's teacher had told April that the other students were afraid of her, that she suspected that April had never been around "these types of children before," and that going to college would be difficult for April, even though this was one of April's biggest goals. When a White student called April the "N word," her teacher refused to punish him and merely told him not to do so again.

April's teacher never contacted her mother to complain about any of April's behaviors. After listening to April speak about her experiences at school on a daily basis, her mother eventually concluded that the teacher didn't really want to deal with April. The fact that April spoke standard English and was an extremely self-confident African American child who was also articulate, tall, a bit overweight for her age, and outspoken were factors that contributed to her problems at school.

2. In your journal, explain
   a. what you would do to help a student like April thrive in your classroom and
   b. what you would do to create a classroom environment that was culturally safe for April and her White classmates.

3. Read the following books and, in your journal, summarize your thoughts, reactions, and ways that you can use this information.
   - *The Little Black Book of Success: Laws of Leadership for Black Women* by Elaine Brown, Marsha Haygood, Rhonda McLean, and Angela Burt-Murray (This book contains excellent leadership strategies, conflict-resolution strategies, and information about cultural differences and racial conflicts that will be beneficial to all teachers, not only African Americans.)
   - *More Courageous Conversations About Race* by Glenn E. Singleton

Part III

Getting Help From the "Village"

How to Maximize Your Relations With Parents, Colleagues, and School Leaders

7 Bridging the Great Divide

How to Create a Win-Win Situation With Parents, *Especially* With Nonwhite Parents

In Part I, Do You *Really* Love *All of Them?* Assessing Your Teaching Self-Confidence About Working With Various Types of Students**, we urged you to examine and improve your teaching self-confidence regarding students' race, gender, socioeconomic status, and academic skills. In **Part II, Student Empowerment–Teacher Empowerment: Increasing Your Teaching Self-Confidence and Your Teaching Efficacy**, we emphasized the importance of improving your classroom management skills and instructional practices and described ways in which you can use the curriculum to improve the racial climate in your classroom. In this section, **Part III, Getting Help From the "Village": How to Maximize Your Relations With Parents, Colleagues, and School Leaders**, we focus on how you can make parents, other teachers, and school leaders your allies and thereby increase your chances of being an outstanding teacher of all students, especially African American students and other students of color. In this chapter, we concentrate on parents first by sharing several short stories and related exercises. Each story is true, but in order to protect their identities, we have changed the names of the parents and their children.

MEET THE PARENT(S) PART 1: A TRADITIONAL FAMILY'S STORY

John, a staff member at a public university, and Maria, an elementary school teacher, appeared to be a model couple. They had a strong marriage, tried to be positive role models to their son and daughter, were active in their Catholic parish, and were hardworking, law-abiding citizens. As a result of the emphasis that they placed on education, their children were well behaved and earned good grades at school. After high school, their daughter earned a graduate degree, and their son earned an engineering degree.

EXERCISE Now It's Your Turn (Part 1)

1. If John and Maria's children were students in your class, how confident do you think you would be in working with their children and why?

_____

_____

_____

_____

2. How confident would you be in meeting with and working with John and Maria and why?

_____

_____

_____

_____

3. In your opinion, what are John and Maria's racial and socioeconomic backgrounds and why?

_____

_____

_____

_____

MEET THE PARENT(S) PART 2:
A COUPLE CHOOSES ADOPTION

Vanessa, a social worker, and Henry, an Army veteran, had a solid marriage and produced two healthy sons. They provided their sons with a loving home life and attempted to instill good values in them. Both boys graduated from high school and eventually married and had children of their own. Although Vanessa was proud of her sons, after they left home, she longed for the daughter that she never had. Consequently, she and Henry decided to adopt a child. When a social worker notified them that a local teenager had recently given birth to a girl who needed to be placed in a permanent home immediately, the couple rushed to the child's foster home. When they saw the baby, it was love at first sight. They had no doubt that this was the child that they'd always wanted. Therefore, they took the newborn home and did their best to give her a good life. Over time, the child excelled in school. When Vanessa had a bout with breast cancer, the girl would hurry home, climb into her mother's bed, read to her, stroke her head, and comfort her. After the cancer went into remission, Vanessa credited her daughter with helping to save her life.

EXERCISE   Now It's Your Turn (Part 2)

1. If Henry and Vanessa's daughter were a student in your class, how confident do you think you would be in working with their daughter and why?

_____

_____

_____

_____

2. How confident would you be in meeting with and working with Henry and Vanessa and why?

_____

_____

_____

_____

3. In your opinion, what are Henry and Vanessa's racial and socioeconomic backgrounds and why?

_____

_____

_____

_____

MEET THE PARENT(S) PART 3: A FAMILY OF IMMIGRANTS

Although they were Laotian, Mrs. Khanthavongsa, along with her adult daughter, son-in-law, and five grandchildren, immigrated to the United States from a refugee camp in Thailand. Even though they had to rely on public assistance to survive in America, when they arrived, they believed that unlimited opportunities awaited them. Mrs. Khanthavongsa wanted her grandchildren to get a good education, especially her little granddaughter, Vanh, who dreamed of attending college and becoming an airline stewardess. However, due to cultural differences and their limited English skills, Mrs. Khanthavongsa's grandchildren had a hard time adjusting to the U.S. public school system. After one day of school, Vanh cried and didn't want to return. Over time, Vanh's older brother gave up on school entirely, joined a gang, and quit school. Mrs. Khanthavongsa often worried about her grandchildren's future, and wondered if moving to America had been the right decision after all.[1]

EXERCISE   Now It's Your Turn (Part 3)

1. If Vanh were a student in your class, how confident would you be in working with her?

_____

_____

_____

_____

2. What specific strategies would you use to help Vanh thrive in your classroom?

_____

_____

_____

_____

3. How confident would you be in meeting with and working with Mrs. Khanthavongsa and Vanh's parents and why?

_____

_____

_____

_____

MEET THE PARENT(S) PART 4: A SINGLE MOTHER'S DILEMMA

Mrs. Amaya was a survivor. Like many Honduran women, she grew up dreaming of marriage and motherhood. When she met and married a man who provided her with a home and eventually fathered three sons with her, it seemed that her dreams had come true. However, like most victims of domestic violence, she never thought that her husband would become abusive, but he did. Her husband was successful and prosperous enough to purchase several real estate properties, but the one thing that he couldn't do was control his temper. After his kicks and punches became too much for her to bear, Mrs. Amaya escaped from Honduras and made her way to the United States. Unfortunately, she left her little boys behind. Now, they became the target of their father's uncontrollable rage.

Seven years after their mother's escape, the boys reached the point where they refused to tolerate their father's abuse. The eldest moved in with a relative. The others, 11-year-old Emilio and 12-year-old Daniel, became street kids who begged, stole, and did whatever they had to in order to eat and survive. Over time, an aunt allowed Emilio to move in with her and telephoned his mother in America. When his mother returned to Honduras, she was virtually a stranger to Emilio. She told her sons that she could only afford to take her youngest son, Emilio, back to the United States with her but promised to send for the others when she could.

When Emilio arrived in the United States, his excitement quickly turned to disappointment. His mother lived in a small apartment with a Mexican family instead of a large house like he had expected. His disappointment increased after his mother lost her job and had to settle for temporary low-paying jobs. Nevertheless, Mrs. Amaya was able to earn enough money to send for her son Daniel to come to the United States. Earning an income; reconnecting with her two sons; and finding ways to feed them, clothe them, help them learn to speak English, and adjust to life in a new country and to the U.S. public school system became her top priorities. Because Daniel appeared to have inherited his father's temper, he and Mrs. Amaya often got into shouting matches. Emilio, on the other hand, quickly began to excel in his English as a second language (ESL) classes. He dreamed of going to college one day and eventually planned to become an attorney or an astronaut.[2]

EXERCISE Now It's Your Turn (Part 4)

1. If you were Daniel's middle school teacher, what strategies would you use to help him thrive in your classroom?

_____

_____

_____

_____

2. If you were Emilio's middle school teacher, what strategies would you use to increase his chances of becoming an attorney or an astronaut?

_____

_____

_____

_____

3. How confident would you be in meeting with and working with Mrs. Amaya and why?

_____

_____

_____

_____

CHAPTER HIGHLIGHTS

Each of the stories that you just read involved one or more parents of color. For example, in the first story, John is a White man, but his wife, Maria, is a Mexican American. The parents in the second story, Henry and Vanessa, are African American. As you know, Mrs. Khanthavongsa was a Laotian immigrant, and Mrs. Amaya emigrated from Honduras. Each parent and guardian had school-age children or grandchildren, and each is a prototype of the type of parents or guardians with whom you may work during your teaching career. Therefore, in this chapter, our goal is to empower you in ways that will help you to view parents as allies and to provide you with information that will enable you to work effectively with all parents, but especially with parents of color. In addition to encouraging you to examine and compare and contrast your views about parents with those of the Teacher Confidence (TC) Study respondents and sharing practical advice and strategies, we share additional stories and facts about parents and guardians. However, before we share some basic facts about the parents and guardians of K–12 students, we'd like for you to measure your teaching self-confidence in more detail.

EXERCISE **Examining Your Teaching Self-Confidence About Working With Parents and Guardians of Pre-K–12 Students**

1. How confident are you about your ability to work effectively with White parents and why?

_____

_____

_____

_____

2. How confident are you about your ability to work effectively with Asian American parents and why?

_____

_____

_____

_____

3. How confident are you about your ability to work effectively with Latino parents and why?

_____

_____

_____

_____

4. How confident are you about your ability to work effectively with African American parents and why?

_____

_____

_____

_____

5. How confident are you about your ability to work effectively with parents who do not speak English and why?

_____

_____

_____

_____

6. Now, examine your answers and summarize what you can learn from them.

_____

_____

_____

_____

Some Basic Facts About the Parents and Guardians of Pre-K–12 Students

- Regardless of their socioeconomic background, most parents and guardians of school-age students want their children to receive a good education.[3]

- Regardless of their race or ethnicity, most parents and guardians of school-age students want their children to receive a good education.[4]

- Regardless of their socioeconomic background, race, or ethnicity, most parents of school-age children are actively involved in their children's education in some way, even when teachers do not see the evidence.[5]

- Teachers often make erroneous assumptions about parents, especially about parents of color.[6]

WHY KNOWING HOW TO WORK EFFECTIVELY WITH ALL PARENTS, ESPECIALLY PARENTS OF COLOR, IS IMPORTANT

Many teachers make their jobs more difficult than necessary by failing to collaborate with parents. Nevertheless, research is clear about the matter: Parent involvement is important, and when parents are highly involved in their children's education, these students are more likely to do well in school.[7] One of the best ways that we can illustrate the importance of parent involvement is to share another true story with you. The story, which I (Gail) heard from Jillian, an African American woman, whom I met on an airplane that was traveling from Georgia to California in 2011, exemplifies what can happen when teachers and parents work together to ensure that a student receives a quality education. We have divided the story into three parts and would like for you to complete related exercises after you read each section.

MEET THE PARENT(S) PART 5, SECTION 1: PARENT INVOLVEMENT THROUGH AN AFRICAN AMERICAN STUDENT'S EYES

Like many parents, Ms. Jackson had big dreams for her children. Although her relationships with the fathers of her son and daughter had not turned out well, she was determined to be an outstanding single mother. According to Jillian, the younger of Ms. Jackson's children, "She was working three jobs. She was working all the time [but] she was always involved."

Ms. Jackson used numerous strategies to help her children. One of her parenting techniques was to constantly emphasize the importance of a good education. "She was always active in our education," Jillian said. "She didn't wait until we got bad grades. As soon as we got a *B* on an assignment, she was on it. She wanted to know why." Ms. Jackson also used ordinary events as opportunities to teach her children life skills and, at the same time, to improve their academic skills. After identifying their strengths and personal preferences, she attempted to turn routine activities into learning experiences. According to Jillian,

> My mom would be in the grocery store, and she would give me the list. She would have me do the shopping, so I had to stay within the budget. She would say, "You have $60 or $100." Then, she would have me help her reconcile her checkbook. . . . It would be like a process. . . . On days when we spent money, she would have me write the [amount] in her checkbook and calculate what the balance was. . . .
>
> At the end of the month, she would get her bank statement. I would go through it with her. We'd go through and see everything that cleared the bank, and see what was outstanding [in order] to get the balance. She was always like that with our learning. She would use it in practical ways.

Unlike Jillian, Ms. Jackson's son, Michael, loved English and language arts assignments. Therefore, Ms. Jackson "would have him proofread stuff," Jillian remarked. "Like if she wrote letters, she would have him edit them. I think that a lot of stuff [like some of the letters] was probably made up. It wasn't going anywhere but the trash."

When her children struggled with schoolwork, Ms. Jackson tutored them. When they excelled, she rewarded them. "If we were doing well, she gave us our independence," Jillian stated.

> If I was getting [high grades], I could do my homework my way. If I got a *C* or a *D*, I had to do it her way. She would make me sit at the table and do it, no distractions. My way [was] I always loved music, so I would do my math homework with my music on.

Although Ms. Jackson believed in rewarding her children for good work, her rewards system had limits. Jillian explained,

> Some parents have to try to bribe their kids with money to do well in school. I asked my mama for money and she was like, "You're doing

what you're supposed to do." She told me "If [you] don't do well in school and get [good] grades, you *really* won't have money when you get older." She told me, "If you don't get [good] grades, then you *really* gonna be broke when you grow older."

One of Ms. Jackson's most effective parenting strategies was to teach her children how to cope with bullies. Because their mother was strict and insisted that her children behave and excel at school, Jillian and Mike were often teased and accused of "acting White." According to Jillian, friends, classmates, and even her cousins teased her "all the time." Jillian explained,

> They would say, "You think you're better than everybody." They would just act like I had to be ghetto to be real, like I wasn't real. I just ignored them because my mom told me, "You're going to lose a lot of friends in trying to be successful." I didn't get beat up though, just comments. Thank God, I didn't get beat up.
>
> I would tell my mom, "People are talking about me because I am tall or because I wear glasses," and she'd say, "So what! Didn't you pick those glasses? Aren't they your favorite glasses? Aren't you good at basketball?" She would always find the positive. She never told me to say anything negative back.

EXERCISE Now It's Your Turn (Part 5, Section 1)

1. Before you read this story, what were your beliefs about African American single mothers and why?

_____

_____

_____

_____

2. What surprised you about this story, and how did the story affect your views about African American parents, especially single mothers?

_____

_____

_____

_____

(Continued)

(Continued)

3. How confident would you be in meeting with and working with Ms. Jackson and why?

_____

_____

_____

_____

MEET THE PARENT(S) PART 5, SECTION 2: PARENT INVOLVEMENT THROUGH AN AFRICAN AMERICAN STUDENT'S EYES

In addition to doing her best at home to help her children earn good grades, Ms. Jackson was very involved at their schools. Because one of her three jobs was a school dispatcher, this made it easy for her to be a visible presence in the school district. However, she also kept in contact with her children's teachers. Jillian said,

> My mom had tabs on me. She would have the teachers' direct phone numbers and she would have them call her directly if I would start to get out of hand. . . . The most important thing my mom did for me was stay involved. My mom just wouldn't let us get away with being bad in class.

Even though Jillian spoke extensively about her mother's positive impact on her, she also wanted me to know that several teachers also did an outstanding job. "So, I had my mom making sure I was taking the classes to go to college," she remarked, "and then, I had two or three supportive teachers, mentors really." One of her favorites was an elementary school teacher. Years later, Jillian had vivid memories of this woman and her effective instructional strategies:

> It was when we were learning the order of operations. . . . maybe third, fourth, or fifth grade. I can't remember. She was so interactive and involved. We watched "School House Rock" videos in class. I still remember songs from that video, like how to multiply. She would make mnemonics and make songs out of them. She would have us play games and we wouldn't even know they were math related until afterward. Instead of just doing math problems, we did math art. If we were doing a diagram, we wouldn't just write it on a piece of paper; we would create posters out of it. She would never call us "stupid." If we didn't understand something, she was very patient.

Jillian also described her two best high school teachers: a woman who taught accounting and a trigonometry teacher. Regarding the trigonometry teacher that she had during her junior year, Jillian explained, "I just had an awesome teacher. She never skipped steps. If we didn't learn something [the previous year], she wouldn't skip it. She would go over it." During Jillian's senior year of high school, she took an accounting class.

It wasn't part of the regular curriculum. I knew about two weeks in that I wanted to be an accountant. I loved the work. I loved the assignments. It was hard stuff, but I just looked forward to doing it, because it was a challenge that I enjoyed. We had a really small class. It was like only 10 people in the class. When we struggled, the teacher could give us one-on-one help that we needed. She recommended me to the Future Business Leaders of America Club on campus, and they would take us to [visit college campuses].

EXERCISE   Now It's Your Turn (Part 5, Section 2)

1. Which characteristics and instructional practices of Jillian's best teachers are most similar to your own?

_____

_____

_____

_____

2. What did you learn from Section 2 of this story that can help you to become a more effective teacher of all students, but especially of African American students and other students of color?

_____

_____

_____

_____

3. In your opinion, how did Jillian turn out as an adult and why?

_____

_____

_____

_____

(Continued)

(Continued)

4. In your opinion, how did Jillian's brother, Michael, turn out as an adult and why?

_____

_____

_____

_____

MEET THE PARENT(S) PART 5, SECTION 3: PARENT INVOLVEMENT THROUGH AN AFRICAN AMERICAN STUDENT'S EYES

The work of Jillian's mother and teachers paid off when Jillian became the first college graduate in her family. At the time when I met her on that California-bound airplane, she was a 27-year-old staff accountant at a health care consulting and accounting firm that was based in Atlanta, where her salary range was $47,000–$50,000 annually. Despite the fact that she loved her job, which required her to compile financial statements, prepare taxes, and advise clients, she had bigger goals. She was already taking courses that would result in a Masters of Business Administration (MBA) degree, and she planned to become a Certified Public Accountant.

Jillian's brother, Michael, had finished high school but "struggled with starting things and never finishing." For a while, he was in the Air Force. He also attended a community college for a period before dropping out. At the time when Jillian and I met on the airplane, her brother had fathered two daughters and had reenrolled in a community college. More importantly, he was following in his mother's footsteps of trying to instill a love and appreciation for a good education in his daughters: a baby and an elementary school student. According to Jillian,

> He's a great father. His two kids have different mothers, but he has my nieces more than the mothers do. Every night, he helps my niece with her homework. She doesn't like math. . . . He takes my niece to new places. When we ask what my niece wants for Christmas, he always wants us to buy books for her, or educational toys. My brother would be devastated if he didn't have his kids.

EXERCISE   Now It's Your Turn (Part 5, Section 3)

1. Now that you have read the entire story, what are the main messages that you can apply to your teaching career from it?

_____

_____

_____

_____

2. Before reading the update about Michael, what were your beliefs about African American male parents, especially single fathers, and why?

_____

_____

_____

_____

3. How confident would you be in meeting with and working with a parent like Michael and why?

_____

_____

_____

_____

We hope that you clearly understand that parent involvement is important and that when parents and teachers strive for academic excellence, positive results can occur. Now, we'd like for you to examine what the TC Study respondents said about working with parents and compare and contrast your views with theirs (see Figure 7.1).

Comments that numerous respondents wrote shed more light on their concerns or lack of concern about working with parents. In explaining, why they rated themselves as *very confident*, for example, several respondents said that the parents' race or language was not a problem. A White female who had taught elementary school for several years wrote, "I feel that I'm confident about my ability to teach/treat all students equally. I also feel confident about my ability to work with parents of all ethnicities." Conversely, some respondents,

Figure 7.1 How the TC Study Participants Rated Their Teaching Self-Confidence About Working With Parents

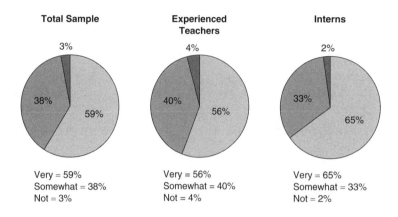

How confident are you about your ability to work effectively with White parents?

Total Sample	Experienced Teachers	Interns
Very = 59%	Very = 56%	Very = 65%
Somewhat = 38%	Somewhat = 40%	Somewhat = 33%
Not = 3%	Not = 4%	Not = 2%

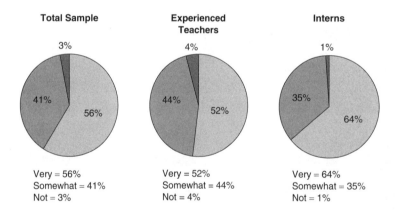

How confident are you about your ability to work effectively with Asian American parents?

Total Sample	Experienced Teachers	Interns
Very = 56%	Very = 52%	Very = 64%
Somewhat = 41%	Somewhat = 44%	Somewhat = 35%
Not = 3%	Not = 4%	Not = 1%

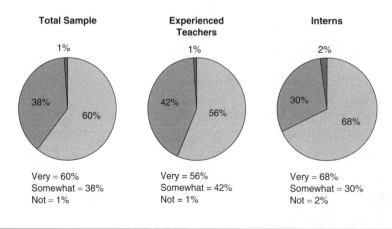

How confident are you about your ability to work effectively with Latino parents?

Total Sample	Experienced Teachers	Interns
Very = 60%	Very = 56%	Very = 68%
Somewhat = 38%	Somewhat = 42%	Somewhat = 30%
Not = 1%	Not = 1%	Not = 2%

Figure 7.1 (Continued)

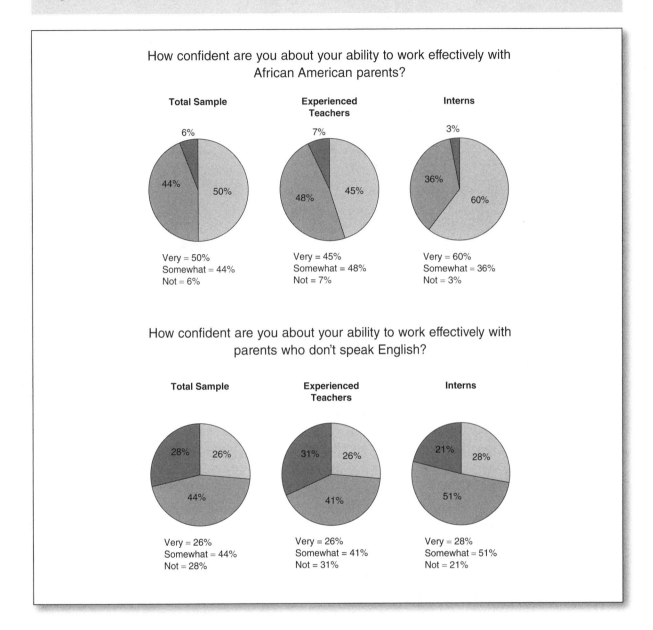

such as an experienced African American elementary teacher who was only somewhat confident about her ability to work effectively with parents, did not have a very high view of parents. She said, "I don't feel that most parents are willing to do what is necessary to ensure success for their children." Similarly, a White male middle school math teacher acknowledged,

> I don't particularly like working with parents. I expect the parents to do their best to provide cooperative and prepared students. When this happens with a good number of my students, I can address the students that need improvement in those areas.

Fear often surfaced as a reason why some respondents lacked confidence about their ability to work effectively with parents. For example, a White female elementary school teacher with one year of teaching experience admitted that she feared "that the parents will judge me because of my race." However, instead of a general fear of parents, most of the related comments were about specific types of parents. In some cases, the fear stemmed from a previous negative experience. For instance, in explaining why she feared African American parents, a Latina who had taught for five years said, "[during an] encounter with an African American parent, I was yelled at and I was scared." In explaining why she felt more confident about her ability to work with African American and Latino parents, rather than White or Asian American parents (whom she equated with having a higher socio-economic status), a White high school English teacher explained,

> I learned I'm afraid of the unknown. Because of my experience working in an urban school, I have not experienced much diversity in my classroom. Our school is composed of two races: Latinos and [B]lacks. I have grown quite comfortable in working with both ethnicities; however . . . what really intimidates me is working with upper-class students and their parents. This is something that I see is changing. I will not always feel this way.

A White female who had taught elementary school for more than five years said that she was only somewhat confident about working with White parents because "[I] worry about parents thinking I am not competent or don't have the ability to [address] their children's specific needs." A White female with more than five years of teaching experience said, "I am afraid of [W]hite parents who are threatened by my curriculum or by my grading system. I avoid contacting non-English-speaking parents because it's so complicated to find a translator."

Although one respondent, a Latina who had taught high school English for one year, admitted, "I feel most comfortable dealing with students and parents of my own race," several respondents did not specify why they were less confident about working with certain groups of parents. An Asian American middle school teacher stated, "I lack confidence in dealing with African American and Latino students or their parents." A White female with less than four years of teaching experience stated, "I don't think I am able to work really effectively with African American parents as I am with other parents."

Other respondents were not necessarily fearful about whether or not they could work effectively with certain groups of parents but lacked confidence, some for specific reasons and others for non- or less-specific reasons. For instance, a White middle school teacher said that she was only somewhat confident about working with African American parents

> because of the aggressive nature of some of them. They may be unwilling to accept the idea that some of the issues may be the child's fault, and the parents need to have the student take responsibility for his/her actions.

Interestingly, an Asian American female intern with no teaching experience but who had worked as a high school math tutor said, "I'm not confident about effectively teaching African Americans, but I am confident about working with African American parents." A White elementary school teacher said that although she was somewhat confident about working with African American parents, "I have not figured out how to communicate with my [English as a] second language parents. I am not very confident."

Many respondents expressed that they were not confident about working with non-English-speaking parents because of communication constraints. A Latina high school teacher wrote, "I do not speak Spanish and am Mexican. I do not know how the parents will judge me." A White high school algebra teacher said,

> I'm not very confident when it comes to working with parents or incorporating racial issues into my lesson plans. I am not at all confident when it comes to working with parents who don't speak English, because I do not speak any other language and don't know how I'll communicate.

EXERCISE   What You Learned From the TC Study Respondents

1. What are the most important points that you learned from the TC Study results and the respondents' answers?

_____

_____

_____

_____

2. Which comments differ from your views and why?

_____

_____

_____

_____

3. Which comments are most similar to your views and why?

_____

_____

_____

_____

CONCLUSION

What We Can Learn From the TC Study

In this chapter, we emphasized that parent involvement is an important predictor of students' academic success. More importantly, when teachers and parents work together, the job of educating students can become much easier for both. However, the TC Study revealed that

- the respondents were more likely to rate themselves as being very confident about their ability to work effectively with Latino parents and White parents than with other racial or ethnic groups of parents;
- the respondents were less likely to rate themselves as being very confident about their ability to work effectively with African American parents than with any other racial or ethnic group of parents.
- the respondents were less likely to rate themselves as being very confident about their ability to work effectively with non-English-speaking parents than with any other category of parents, and that
- fear and previous negative experiences contributed to some respondents' lack of confidence about their ability to work with parents effectively.

Therefore, even if you are very confident about your ability to work effectively with parents, regardless of their background, the TC Study results indicate that many experienced teachers struggle in this area. For this reason, it is in your best interest to arm yourself with as many strategies as possible to increase your chances of forming strong relationships with your students' parents. The following strategies, stories, and professional growth exercises are designed to assist you.

ADVICE AND STRATEGIES

1. Increase your confidence level by practicing.

As the old saying goes, "Practice makes perfect." Practice can also help you to become more confident about your ability to work effectively with parents. One way that you can practice is to ask your friends and family members to pretend that they are the parents of your students and practice what you would like to say on them. Then ask them for feedback. You can also create videos of yourself and a close friend or relative engaging in mock parent meetings and then review and critique the videos to strengthen your skills. A simpler way is to merely sit in front of a mirror and practice alone.

Furthermore, before you contact a parent about a student's misbehavior or another problem, make sure that you know exactly what you want to say. In this situation, practicing ahead of time can really boost your confidence. You can use the following scripts that Yvette Rosales Coria, a school staff member and my (Rufus's) former assistant, created or modify them to suit your needs:

Parent Script 1

Hello, (insert the parent's name). My name is (insert your name), and I'm calling from (insert the name of your school). The reason I'm calling is that I have your child, (insert the student's name), in my (insert information about your class) and I was wondering if you could help me resolve a problem. Today, (insert student's name) refused to do (his or her) class work and kept talking to other students when (he or she) should have been working. I really want to help (insert student's name) succeed in my class, but I need your help.

Parent Script 2

Hello, (insert the parent's name). My name is (insert your name), and I'm calling from (Insert the name of your school). The reason I'm calling is that I have your child, (insert the student's name), in my (insert information about your class) and I need your help. Today, (insert student's name) was extremely disrespectful to me by (explain what the student said or did). This behavior is totally unacceptable, and I need your help in resolving this matter.

2. Form a blog or some other method of communicating with teachers and school support staff about parent involvement.

Creating a blog will give you a forum whereby you can receive suggestions from others about how you and other teachers can improve your relationships with parents, work more effectively with parents, and increase parent involvement. The personal stories, questions, and strategies that the audience will share can be beneficial to you and the other bloggers. Moreover, many of the bloggers will probably be actual parents of K–12 students who can write from their own personal experiences with teachers. However, make sure that you don't put any confidential or libelous information about a student or parent on the blog that could result in a lawsuit against you.

3. Contact parents early in the school year.

Instead of waiting for parents to contact you or waiting until you are forced to contact a parent because of a student's misbehavior, soon after the school term begins, send a note or letter home to parents. Introduce yourself, provide your contact information, explain your expectations, invite parents to contact you, and ask parents what they expect from you. If you know that some of the parents are non-English speakers, ask a school leader on campus or at the district level to recommend someone who can translate the letter into the parent's language. Here's an example of a sample letter:

Sample Letter to Parents

Dear Parent or Guardian:

I am excited that your child is a student in my fourth grade class this year. During the first week of school, your child brought home a document that explained my goals/objectives, class rules, grading policy, and policy concerning missed or late assignments. This document required your signature. If you would like another copy of it or if you would like to contact me for any reason, please telephone me, e-mail me, or send a note with your child. I look forward to working closely with you to help your child have an outstanding school year. I would also like to know what you expect from me. Please write your expectations, any information that you would like for me to know about your child, and any suggestions that you have at the bottom of or on the back of this letter.

Sincerely: _____ Date: _____

E-mail: _____ Telephone: _____

Comments: _____

_____

_____

_____

---

4. Identify the active parents at your school site.

You can also take advantage of the fact that many parents are visibly active at various school events and are often on campus. Some of these parents will have a good reputation with school personnel, but others may be viewed as meddlers. Both groups of parents can give you invaluable advice if you find ways to meet and connect with them. Regardless of what other school personnel say or think, form your own opinions, because the parent with the worst reputation may become your biggest ally and give you insights about the school and local community that you would not know otherwise.

5. Get connected to the community in which your school is located.

The most difficult thing for me (Rufus) when I was teaching teachers or future teachers at the university level was working with second-career folks who thought that they were going to go into teaching because it was easier than what they had done before their career change. I would be candid with these potential teachers and tell them that they were entering the wrong profession if they thought they were going to work less. Teachers should care about the children and about the community in which they teach. This is true for you also; you should be connected to the community where your school is located. Just because you don't live there doesn't mean you shouldn't invest time there. If it isn't possible for you to do so, then spend more time with the students when you can. The community will appreciate you if you show that you care. Parents and their children need to know that you are striving to make sure their children receive the best education you can deliver.

6. Learn what you can from seemingly negative experiences and apologize when necessary.

One of the many conversations I (Rufus) had with my colleagues over the years in a California school district—which had an African American population of about 14 percent at the time—was very powerful. A White teacher asked if she could speak with me. She was hurting emotionally because a parent had called her a racist. Often, when this happens, people in leadership, teachers, administrators, politicians, and law enforcement become uncomfortable and accuse the person of color of "playing the race card." The real issue, however, is that instead of trying to identify the core issues or problems, these individuals dismiss the concerns of the person of color. Unlike these individuals, my colleague wanted to know why it happened.

It turned out that the African American parent was justifiably concerned that her child was being targeted by the White teacher. When I began to ask my colleague questions about what had happened, she started crying. It turned out that when other students in her class raised their hand repeatedly or yelled out, she said that she would deal with them in a fair manner, but after I asked her additional questions, her countenance changed. She realized that she had indeed been singling out the African American student. For this reason, she became very apologetic. She was remorseful and explained, "I did not grow up around Black people. I did not go to college with Black people. I come to work to teach and think I am going to love my kids, and I do. But I look at my class of 24 children and 10 of them look nothing like me."

Like many educators, this teacher had not done her student teaching in a culturally diverse school, and she'd had virtually no opportunities to work with students of color. Therefore, in her own classroom, she did what most human beings would do; she reverted to what she knew: stereotypes. During our conversation, she said such things to me as, "We need Black people for music and entertainment." When I asked if this is what she had said to the African American parent, she said, "Yes!" Of course, the parent was offended.

I recommended that the teacher search for diversity programs on her own. I explained why it took 10 years for Bill Cosby to get a television show about two professional African American parents who were raising wonderful children when the only programs on at the time were comedies, which often demeaned African American males. The reason was stereotypes and a failure to realize that African Americans have diverse beliefs, socioeconomic backgrounds, experiences, levels of education, and professions. Furthermore, I suggested the following strategies that may also be useful to you.

What to Do if a Parent Accuses You of Being Racist

- Call the parent as soon as possible and apologize if you have behaved in a culturally insensitive or racist manner.

- Inform the parent that you honestly did not realize that you were singling his or her child out (or engaging in another specific type of offensive behavior).

- Tell the parent that you appreciate the fact that the parent brought the problem to your attention.

- Invite the parent to visit your classroom and even participate in class activities.

Later that year, the teacher and I had a follow-up conversation. With a huge smile on her face, she informed me that she was enjoying her African American students. Over time, she did become an excellent teacher and, later, an excellent administrator.

7. Familiarize yourself with additional strategies to use with non-English-speaking parents.

In *How to Reach Out to Parents of ELLs*, educator Pat Mora suggests that (a) educators find bilingual school staff who can serve as translators, (b) that educators improve their Spanish skills, and (c) that educators provide parents with information that will help them to better understand the U.S. school system, teacher expectations, and the resources that are available to parents.[8] In *How to Communicate With Non-English Speaking Parents,* Judith Willson urges educators to use online translation programs to learn "simple phrases in the parents' language" and to provide parents with feedback.[9] *A Guide for Engaging ELL Families: Twenty Strategies for School Leaders* describes ways in which educators can connect with, communicate with, and improve the involvement of ELL parents.[10]

APPLYING WHAT YOU LEARNED TO YOUR *YES, I CAN!* JOURNAL

1. Read the following story from Rufus's teaching experiences.

A parent of two of my (Rufus's) African American students who were brothers kept complaining about me to my school principal. According to this parent, his sons were coming home saying that "Mr. Thompson is picking on us." On several occasions, I had contacted the parents—primarily the father—about the boys' behaviors in my classes. At the time, our middle school was pretty small, so I had the boys in three of my classes: physical education, social studies, and reading. Mr. Shumway, the principal and my mentor, was keeping me informed about the situation. However, when he told me that the boys' father thought I was a racist, I was shocked.

Each year, our school used to have a big community carnival to raise money for our clubs. We would raise thousands of dollars and the community would come out and have a great time. That year, I was one of the coordinators of the carnival. At some point, Mr. Shumway approached me and said, "Mr. Thompson, I would like for you to meet [the boys' father]." The parent looked at me, smiled, and said, "Hello, Mr. Thompson." We began to discuss his sons' behaviors and my way of handling them. He knew his boys well, and he also realized that the type of complaints that they were coming home with were based on an effort on my part to teach them the same manners and respect that he and his wife were instilling in them. I was treating them the same way in which I was treating the other kids, but I was also stricter on them. Without realizing it, I had been using a stereotypical, institutional-racism model that is based on the dangerous notion that being overly strict and punitive are the best ways to prevent African American males from becoming criminals. During our conversation, the father helped me to realize this. Therefore, I decided to change my approach to make sure that I wasn't being stricter on African American males than on other students. At the end of the conversation, the father assured me, "You will not have any more trouble out of my boys."

Not only did I become more aware of how I was treating those young men, but I also became a better teacher. It took a White, Mormon principal and an African American parent to enlighten me. However, if I had not been willing to listen, I would never have grown as a teacher, and as a result, I could have unknowingly damaged countless African American male students.

2. In your journal, explain
   a. the ways in which this story can help you to work more effectively with parents,
   b. what you can do if a parent accuses you of being racist, and
   c. how you will hold yourself accountable for not being overly strict on African American males or on any student.

3. Read the following works and, in your journal, summarize the lessons/messages that can help you work more effectively with parents.
   • *My Years as a Hispanic Youth Advocate . . . and the Lessons I Have Learned* by Barbara L. Lovejoy

- "To Be Honest: I Can't Stand His Mama: Facing Your Personal Issues About the Parents of African American Students" in *The Power of One: How You Can Help or Harm African American Students* by Gail L. Thompson
- "Yes! They Do Care About My Education: Parent Involvement in Schools" in *Up Where We Belong: Helping African American and Latino Students Rise in School and in Life* by Gail L. Thompson
- The Colorín Colorado website: (http://www.colorincolorado.org/index .php?langswitch = en). Visit this site to find many resources that can help you increase your efficacy with ELL students and work effectively with their parents.

Ties That Can Bind 8

Forming Strong Working Relationships With Colleagues of Color

In Chapter 1, we introduced you to Michaela, a beginning teacher who worked at an urban high school in a low-income community. The following story, which Michaela shared with us by telephone and e-mail, is based on an experience that she had during the summer after her second year of teaching. As you read it, please complete the related exercises.

MICHAELA AND HER COLLEAGUE: "NO ONE WANTS TO LOOK UP WORDS IN THE DICTIONARY FOR THREE HOURS" (PART 1)

At the end of her second year of teaching, in order to fulfill one of the requirements to earn a master's degree in education, Michaela needed to complete several classroom observations and teach a class session in a more experienced teacher's classroom. Therefore, in May 2013, she asked a colleague in her department if she could visit the remedial summer school class the woman was teaching. Michaela selected this teacher, a middle-aged White woman, because she had been friendly and helpful during Michaela's first two years of teaching. When her colleague told her that she was welcome to visit her summer school class—which was supposed to prepare incoming ninth graders for high school—as often as needed and agreed to permit her to teach a class session, Michaela was thrilled. However, things soon went downhill.

On the first day that Michaela visited her colleague's classroom, she quickly realized that the teacher and students appeared to have a hostile relationship. While the students were within earshot, the teacher informed her, "These are really low [achieving] kids. I have all the far-below-basic kids, so they're really low." Furthermore, according to Michaela,

[her colleague] accused [students] of stealing her colored pens, but the missing pens were in the classroom; one was even on the teacher's desk. She'd overreact to kids stretching or taking too long to get to their seats. She spoke to them in condescending tones about everything!

During each classroom visit, Michaela's frustration grew. She explained,

[The teacher] tried to teach them root words, prefixes, and how to use the dictionary. She also tried to use short stories, but it was unclear what she was trying to teach with those. I think she was trying to model reading strategies. She used the "Think Aloud" strategy, but she used "reading specialist" jargon, so it was boring on top of going over the kids' heads.

She said, "Gary's special ed.," right in front of Gary, who was a brilliant gifted special education kid who'd probably just had a bad test year. She constantly talked to me about their "bad behavior" and told me, "They won't do anything!" right in front of all the kids.

Like Michaela, the students were also frustrated. Michaela said,

The students were subtly defiant, refusing to do work. But I suspect it's because they didn't know how to do it, since she was terrible at explaining things. That, or they weren't interested, because no one wants to look up words in the dictionary for three hours. No one.

EXERCISE   Now It's Your Turn (Part 1)

1. What are your overall thoughts about the first part of this story?

_____

_____

_____

_____

2. How can this story help you to become a more effective teacher of all students, especially of students of color?

_____

_____

_____

_____

3. In your opinion, what specific steps could the regular teacher take to improve her relations with the students?

_____

_____

_____

_____

MICHAELA AND HER COLLEAGUE: "NO ONE WANTS TO LOOK UP WORDS IN THE DICTIONARY FOR THREE HOURS" (PART 2)

When the day arrived for Michaela to teach the class, her colleague warned her to expect the worst: apathy and misbehavior. After all, this is how the students had behaved with her from the beginning of summer school onward. In spite of this warning, Michaela did her best to prepare to have a positive experience. She recounted,

> My lesson was on "characterization." I started by saying my only rules were that they pay attention and didn't speak while I was speaking. I showed them a video clip of "The Little Red Hen." Then, I asked them to tell me things they heard the little red hen say and do, what she thought, and how others treated her. They gave me examples for each, and I filled out a graphic organizer with the information they provided. Then, I asked them what each piece of information they provided said about the little red hen's personality. I told them, "Those are called *character traits*, and they can be inferred based on what characters say, do, and think, and what others say about that character."
>
> Next, I referred them to the story they read with their teacher the day before. I asked them to repeat the process for the main character. After that, I asked them to write a paragraph analyzing the character. I gave them sentence frames for that part, and they got to work in pairs. Two groups ran out of time. The rest finished that day. They were nice and respectful.

[Afterward], the teacher was salty. She had a scowl on her face and didn't really acknowledge me when I left. She's usually very nice to me. [After all], she came to my wedding and gave us $100. So she was clearly mad that I had success with the kids after she'd warned me that some of them would refuse to do my work and that there would be behavior problems. Her approach was wrong, and no one likes a condescending [W]hite lady.

EXERCISE   Now It's Your Turn (Part 2)

1. Now that you have read both sections, what are your overall thoughts about the entire story?

_____

_____

_____

_____

2. How can this story help you to become a more effective teacher of all students, especially of students of color?

_____

_____

_____

_____

3. Explain why you agree or disagree with Michaela's statement, "[The teacher] was clearly mad that I had success with the kids after she'd warned me that some of them would refuse to do my work and that there would be behavior problems."

_____

_____

_____

_____

4. Explain why you agree or disagree with Michaela's statement, "Her approach was wrong, and no one likes a condescending [W]hite lady."

_____

_____

_____

_____

5. How can this story help you to strengthen your relations with your colleagues?

_____

_____

_____

_____

CHAPTER HIGHLIGHTS

In the previous chapter, we emphasized the importance of working with parents to ensure optimum student success. In this chapter, our goal is to convince you to find ways to form strong professional bonds with White teachers and with teachers of color. Although the Teacher Confidence (TC) Study did not include statements about working with colleagues, the research that we share will underscore the reasons why your colleagues can become an invaluable resource for you. As in previous chapters, we share stories, advice and strategies, professional growth exercises, recommended readings, and research. In the next section, we would like for you to complete another confidence examination exercise.

EXERCISE   Examining Your Confidence Levels About Working With Other Teachers

1. How confident are you about your ability to collaborate with and form strong positive relationships with White teachers at your school site and in your school district and why?

_____

_____

_____

_____

2. How confident are you about your ability to collaborate with and form strong positive relationships with Asian American teachers at your school site and in your school district and why?

_____

_____

_____

_____

(Continued)

(Continued)

3. How confident are you about your ability to collaborate with and form strong positive relationships with Latino teachers at your school site and in your school district and why?

_____

_____

_____

_____

4. How confident are you about your ability to collaborate with and form strong positive relationships with African American teachers at your school site and in your school district and why?

_____

_____

_____

_____

5. Now, review your answers and (a) explain what they reveal about you and (b) describe areas on which you need to work.

_____

_____

_____

_____

Some Basic Facts About the K–12 Public Schools' Teaching Force

The following facts come from the National Center for Education Statistics in 2011:

- There were over 3 million K–12 teachers in U.S. schools.
- Females made up nearly 80 percent of the K–12 teaching force.
- Approximately 40 percent of the K–12 teaching force was younger than 40 years old.
- Slightly more than half of the K–12 teaching force had a master's degree or higher degree.
- Whites accounted for approximately 80 percent of the K–12 teaching force.
- Blacks made up approximately 7 percent of the K–12 teaching force.

- Hispanics accounted for approximately 7 percent of the K–12 teaching force.

- Asian Americans made up approximately 1 percent of the K–12 teaching force.

- Mixed-race educators accounted for approximately 1 percent of the K–12 teaching force.

- Pacific Islanders made up less than 1 percent of the K–12 teaching force.

- American Indians and Alaska Natives accounted for less than 1 percent of the K–12 teaching force.[1]

WHY STRENGTHENING YOUR RELATIONS WITH WHITE TEACHERS AND ESPECIALLY WITH COLLEAGUES OF COLOR IS IMPORTANT

By now, you know that teaching can be a rewarding yet difficult job. In addition to finding ways to prepare and deliver lessons that will provide your students with an outstanding education, you will also have to find ways to work well with parents. Furthermore, you will also have to deal with other teachers in your department, with teachers who teach the same grade level(s) you teach, and possibly even with those who teach other grade levels and who teach in other departments. At the very least, you can choose to do the bare minimum and only interact with your colleagues when necessary and on a superficial level. On the other hand, you can choose to view your colleagues, especially your colleagues of color, as an additional resource that can make your job easier and as a resource that can provide you with information that can help you increase your efficacy with all students, particularly with students of color.

Just as students often enjoy interacting with their classmates and student collaboration is a highly touted effective educational strategy, research indicates that teacher collaboration is important. One report, *Primary Sources 2012: America's Teachers on the Teaching Profession*, which was based on feedback from more than 10,000 teachers, indicated that 89 percent of the teachers said that having time to collaborate was "absolutely essential" or "very important." Moreover, 53 percent said that having "in-school teaching mentors/coaches for the first three years of teaching" was "absolutely essential" or "very important."[2] Although the average teacher in the study spent about 15 minutes collaborating with colleagues each day, most said they believed that more time should be spent on collaboration.[3]

In the MetLife Survey of the American Teacher report, *Collaborating for Student Success*, which involved over 1,000 public school teachers, 500 school principals, and more than 1,000 students, the majority of teachers and principals agreed "that greater collaboration among teachers and school leaders would have a major impact on improving student achievement"; the study also found that the average teacher spent "2.7 hours per week in structured collaboration with other teachers and school leaders." Nearly one quarter of the teachers spent "more than 3 hours per week" collaborating with the other teachers and school leaders.[4] Furthermore, the authors of this study identified the three most commonly cited types of collaboration: "teachers meeting in teams to learn what is necessary to help their students achieve at higher levels; school leaders sharing responsibility with teachers to achieve school goals; and beginning teachers working with more experienced teachers."[5]

Despite the fact that the research suggests that many teachers want to collaborate with their colleagues and believe that collaboration is important, the research also indicates that many teachers are dissatisfied about the level of support that they receive from their colleagues. For example, in *Lessons Learned: New Teachers Talk About Their Jobs, Challenges, and Long-Range Plans* (which we cited in previous chapters), the majority of the beginning teachers were satisfied with the support that they received from their colleagues, but many were not. In fact, "[j]ust a quarter of new high school and middle school teachers (26 percent) say they get excellent advice from fellow teachers on lesson plans and teaching techniques, compared with 39 percent of elementary school teachers. There is a similar 10-point spread on the advice they get about handling unmotivated or misbehaving students."[6]

Another problem is a lack of collaboration across racial lines. The fact that teachers of color are extremely underrepresented in the K–12 teaching force means that throughout the United States, many teachers work in schools in which they have few, if any, colleagues of color. Nevertheless, teachers of color are extremely important to the education system. For this reason, higher education officials at colleges and universities often make a concerted effort to recruit students of color into teaching programs. Moreover, Secretary of Education Arne Duncan made diversifying the teaching corps a national priority. According to Duncan, teachers of color can have a positive effect on student morale, student effort, and student achievement. In a CNN interview with Steve Perry, a nationally renowned high school principal, Duncan spoke specifically about his efforts to recruit more Black males into the teaching force. According to Duncan,

> Far too few of our teachers look like our children. . . . I think students need great teachers of whatever color, but I will tell you that I've seen African American male teachers have a profound, profound impact on young men who are desperately looking for father figures.[7]

In spite of the small number of teachers of color in many U.S. schools, we urge you to view teachers of color as colleagues who can help you increase your efficacy with all students, but especially with students of color. In a study titled *Teacher Diversity Matters: A State-by-State Analysis of Teachers of Color*, the author, Ulrich Boser, stated,

> Teachers of color serve as role models for students, giving them a clear and concrete sense of what diversity in education—and in our society—looks like. A recent review of empirical studies also shows that students of color do better on a variety of academic outcomes if they're taught by teachers of color.[8]

Therefore, teachers of color can broaden your understanding of cultural diversity; help you to better understand students of color; help you to better understand parents of color; and provide you with tips, advice, and strategies that can empower you. The two stories that follow and the related examples illustrate these points. The first story is about a young White elementary school teacher (whose name has been changed). This teacher developed good relationships with an African American instructional aide and with an African American school principal. The second story is about a White teacher and me (Rufus) during the time that I was a middle school teacher.

A WHITE TEACHER GETS CALLED THE "R WORD" BY AN AFRICAN AMERICAN PARENT (PART 1)

Ms. Novack, a young White woman, taught kindergarten at an elementary school in eastern North Carolina. In 2013, the city where the school is located was 70 percent White and 26 percent African American. Although mixed-race residents made up slightly more than 1 percent of the population, Latinos, Asian Americans, and American Indians made up less than 1 percent each. Therefore, most of the students of color in Ms. Novack's class were African Americans. Surprisingly, in a city that was overwhelming White, her instructional aide and the principal of the school were African Americans.

   Like most beginning teachers, Ms. Novack wanted her students to excel academically. So she worked hard to create good lesson plans. Even though she wanted them to have fun while learning, providing them with a curriculum that would prepare them for first grade was never far from her mind. Therefore, because of her high expectations, dedication, and love for teaching, in 2012, Ms. Novack was shocked when an African American parent accused her of being racist.

E X E R C I S E   What You Learned From Ms. Novack's Story (Part 1)

1. In your opinion, what may have caused a parent to accuse a hardworking, dedicated kindergarten teacher of being racist?

_____

_____

_____

_____

2. If you were Ms. Novack, how would you handle this situation?

_____

_____

_____

_____

A WHITE TEACHER GETS CALLED THE "R WORD" BY AN AFRICAN AMERICAN PARENT (PART 2)

As expected, Ms. Novack was devastated when the parent accused her of being racist. She believed that she had treated the woman's child fairly and believed that she had never engaged in any type of racist or offensive behavior toward that student or any other student. But she had no idea how she could convince the parent that she was not a racist.

When she informed her instructional aide and the school principal of the hurtful allegation, both were outraged. Instead of siding with the angry parent, they defended Ms. Novack. Both knew this teacher well, were certain that she was an outstanding teacher, and knew that she treated her students fairly. Because a teacher with a stellar reputation had been falsely accused, the principal took matters into her own hands. She not only contacted the parent and told her that she was wrong for labeling Ms. Novack as a racist, but she also told the parent "Your child is a spoiled brat!" From this point on, Ms. Novack did not have any problems with the parent.

EXERCISE **What You Learned From Ms. Novack's Story (Part 2)**

1. What lessons can you learn from this story?

_____

_____

_____

_____

2. How might this story have ended if Ms. Novack had not developed positive relationships with her instructional aide and the principal?

_____

_____

_____

_____

AN AFRICAN AMERICAN TEACHER AND WHITE TEACHER FORM A DECADES-LONG FRIENDSHIP (PART 1)

At the beginning of my (Rufus's) eighth year of teaching middle school, Lane Rankin, a young White male, was hired to teach math at our school. He was friendly, enthusiastic, and exuded positive energy. As the only African American teacher at a predominantly White school, I had no idea when I met Lane that he and I would eventually become not only good colleagues but best friends.

During the period when Lane was hired, I had pretty much withdrawn into my own professional world. My students were my top priority and I was determined to do my best. I behaved in a collegial manner with my colleagues but had developed few, if any, real friendships by choice. But despite the fact that our upbringings and racial backgrounds were very different, Lane changed my career and my life. As I got to know him better, his zeal for knowledge as it applies to teaching students, his fresh approach to learning, and his thinking outside the box reminded me of my early teaching years. Because I was a technology pioneer in the field of education, Lane's attitude and teaching style inspired me. He was able to get students excited about math and life, and throughout his teaching career, he used technology to enhance the math experiences of thousands of middle school students.

One example of his innovative teaching style was a lesson on ratios and proportions. Because he always wanted his lessons to be practical and realistic, he divided students into groups and had them use gummy bears candy to solve math problems over several class periods. After inputting data into a spreadsheet, one group discovered that there was a disproportionate number of a particular color of gummy bears. When they realized that this conflicted with what the candy manufacturer had stated, the students drafted a letter based on their findings, and Lane sent the letter to the company. To the students' delight, the company sent a certificate and coupons to them.

I could tell you many stories about Lane. We had a great time providing our students with an interesting and challenging curriculum that they could use in real life. Over time, Lane went on to inspire other new teachers, as did I. When there is a great teacher around, other teachers benefit. When an older teacher starts to lose his or her enthusiasm for teaching, a teacher like Lane can inspire that teacher. The best part is that the older teacher's students will become more enthusiastic as well.

EXERCISE   What You Learned From Rufus and Lane's Story (Part 1)

1. In your opinion, why were Lane and I (Rufus) able to develop a long-term friendship when we came from such different backgrounds?

_____

_____

_____

_____

(Continued)

(Continued)

2. What are some similarities and differences between Lane and you?

_____

_____

_____

_____

AN AFRICAN AMERICAN TEACHER AND WHITE TEACHER FORM A DECADES-LONG FRIENDSHIP (PART 2)

In case you're wondering how and why Lane and I were able to develop a lasting friendship, here's the answer: During our conversations, we learned that although there were many differences between us, our philosophies and beliefs were very similar. I grew up segregated geographically from Whites as a result of de facto segregation in Fontana, California, in the 1960s and 1970s. Nevertheless, because I was an athlete, I was a recipient of the overwhelming kindness of progressive White people in Fontana, who basically protected me from the bigotry and racism in that city and put their reputations on the line doing it. Lane grew up in a similar city. We both loved the cities in which we grew up. Our experiences as they apply to race were and still are totally different. That is what many White people don't understand. People of color have to be able to see more of the picture than Whites because of the way our society is designed. It is an ingrained design.

Today, I believe that God put us together. At the time when he was hired at our school, I needed him more than he needed me. Before he arrived, I got along with my White colleagues, because that is who I am. People in general liked me and considered me their friend, but in reality, I viewed my circle of friends as consisting of about 10 people. Therefore, when I was at work, I interacted with people, but when I went home, I interacted with my family and people in my neighborhood. My family away from home was the teachers and staff whom I worked with but I didn't do much socially with them. But Lane was different. To me, he seemed like a man who took the chances that I wanted to take but couldn't because I didn't have the vision or the skills that he had.

As I got to know him more, I learned that he loved his grandmother deeply, and I had been raised by my grandmother. The conversations that we had and the similarities that surfaced were the underpinnings that resulted in a great friendship. At the same time, as we bounced ideas off each other, discussed innovative instructional strategies, and promoted the use of technology in our classrooms, our reputations for being exemplary teachers spread. As a result, during our years as middle school teachers, we had many great times traveling throughout California in order to train educators on how to use and implement technology into their curricula. So the strong friendship and brotherhood that we share today grew out of the many conversations and collaborative work that we did during that period.

Even though Lane left teaching to become a CEO and an internationally renowned educational software developer and I am now a retired educator, our close friendship has flourished. Because we dared to venture out of our comfort zones, were willing to have difficult conversations about race and other issues, and learned when to agree and when to disagree respectfully, our friendship has evolved into a brotherhood.

EXERCISE   What You Learned From Rufus and Lane's Story (Part 2)

1. In your opinion, what are the most important messages in this story?

_____

_____

_____

_____

2. Make a list of teachers at your school site whom you would like to get to know better and the reasons why.

_____

_____

_____

_____

CONCLUSION

Collaborating with your colleagues and forming strong professional relationships with them can strengthen your teaching skills and help you work more effectively with all students. Because the K–12 public school teaching force is predominantly White and female, most of your fellow teachers will fit into these categories. However, although there are only a small number of teachers of color at many schools, we urge you to understand that these teachers can help you to grow in ways that may increase your efficacy with students of color. The following tips are designed to help you reach out to teachers of color.

ADVICE AND STRATEGIES

1. Be courageous.

During your first years of teaching, it might be easier to wait until teachers of color, especially teachers of color who have more teaching experience than you do, approach you, rather than approaching them first. However, if you choose to take the first step, you may find that your colleague is eager to work with you. You will never know until you try. Therefore, we urge you to muster up your courage and make a commitment to reach out. You can use the following script as an ice breaker, modify it to suit your comfort level, or create one of your own and practice it before you test it on a colleague:

Connecting With Colleagues Script

Hi,

My name is _____. I am relatively new to teaching and am eager to learn as much as I can. Would you be interested in sharing ideas and suggestions with me about how I can work more effectively with students at this school and with their parents?

---

2. Try different approaches.

There are many ways that you can reach out to your colleagues of color. Introducing yourself is a simple first step. Inviting a colleague to visit your classroom to offer feedback is another. Asking a colleague if you can visit his or her classroom to observe this teacher's teaching style and practices is another. You can also ask a colleague to have lunch with you in order to get to know him or her better and ask for help in solving a problem with a particular student or parent.

3. Be discerning.

In your efforts to form strong positive professional relationships with your colleagues of color, it is important to also remember to be discerning and self-protective. People of color are humans, just as Whites are. Therefore, you may encounter some who carry negative mental baggage about students of color and their parents. You can tell by their behavior, what they say, and what students say about them. A colleague who speaks negatively about students and parents, uses stereotypes, and clearly has low expectations for students of color is not going to help you grow as an educator. Search for individuals who have a positive attitude about teaching, students, and parents and who are willing to help you strengthen your skills and expand your knowledge base.

4. Stay out of the toxic place(s) on campus.

Every school site appears to have a classroom or some other place where negative, burned-out, and sometimes even racist teachers congregate. Often, it happens to be the staff/teachers' lounge. Make sure that you avoid this place. I (Gail) have seen new teachers who hang out with this negative crowd transform from being optimistic and energetic individuals at the beginning of the school year into bitter teachers who are hopeless about students and parents at the end of the year. As the old saying goes, "If you lie down with dogs, you'll rise up with fleas." I often ate lunch in my classroom alone because I got tired of hearing certain colleagues brag about the number of students who had failed their classes, complain about how lazy the students were, or insist that the students' parents did not care about their children's academic welfare. I agree with the saying that "It is better to be alone than in bad company." However, over time and by being discerning, I learned that many of my colleagues were wonderful teachers who had not lost hope. These were the teachers who could help me grow. Therefore, I sought to cultivate positive relationships with them.

Conversely, my (Rufus's) experience was different. For many years, I was the only teacher of color at my school site. We were a small school staff who all ate lunch in the same location. This means that I heard a lot of negative comments about students of color and their parents. During the times when I did hear offensive remarks and stereotypes that a few teachers felt were okay to say in front of me, I listened and kept quiet. However, those comments and attitudes made me work even harder to make sure that my students did not fit the stereotypes that some teachers had about them.

5. Be proactive.

If you teach at a school where there are few or no teachers of color, there are other ways to form professional relationships with teachers of color. Seeking out teachers of color at other schools in your district is one way to do this. Attending educational conferences and professional development workshops is another. Joining organizations for educators that have racially diverse memberships is another. Starting a blog or joining blogs for teachers is an option as well.

6. Go to the experts.

Countless researchers and educators of color have devoted their careers to creating works that are designed to improve race relations, improve the schooling experiences of students of color, help educators work more effectively with parents of color, and broaden educators' cultural awareness. Familiarizing yourself with their work is one of the best ways for you to learn how to become a more effective educator of students of color. Throughout this book, we have recommended some of these works. Reading these works and searching the bibliographies for additional great books and articles can enable you to better understand your colleagues of color as well. More importantly, this knowledge can provide you with the foundation to eventually become a mentor teacher to other beginning teachers.

APPLYING WHAT YOU LEARNED TO YOUR *YES, I CAN!* JOURNAL

1. Summarize the most important points that you would like to remember from this chapter.

2. Read the following works and, in your journal, summarize the lessons/messages that can help you work more effectively with your colleagues, especially with colleagues of color.

    *   *Becoming Multicultural Educators: Personal Journey Toward Professional Agency* edited by Geneva Gay
    *   *The Best for Our Children: Critical Perspectives on Literacy for Latino Students* edited by Maria de la Luz Reyes and John J. Halcon
    *   *Up Against Whiteness: Race, School, and Immigrant Youth* by Stacey J. Lee
    *   *Beyond the Big House: African American Educators on Teacher Education* by Gloria Ladson-Billings
    *   *Growing Up White: A Veteran Teacher Reflects on Racism* by Julie Landsman

Ask and It Might Be Given 9

Getting What You Need From School Leaders

This chapter is designed to help you strengthen your relations with school leaders, regardless of their racial or ethnic background. We begin with a three-part story about a White K–12 female school principal and an African American male student. After you read each part of the story, please complete the related exercise.

A PRINCIPAL'S DILEMMA (PART 1)

On an ordinary school day in 2013, Ms. Smith, who had been an elementary school principal in New Jersey for many years, was strolling down a hallway when she heard a commotion in the school cafeteria. When she entered, several children began to yell, "Lamar stole Anthony's cell phone!" Lamar, an African American 10-year-old, shouted, "No, I didn't! I didn't do it." Ms. Smith had to decide how to proceed. Whom should she believe: the students who were insisting that Lamar had stolen the cell phone or Lamar, a student who had never been in trouble at school before? After all, Lamar came from a stable family. His mother was a homemaker, his father often worked from home, and the family lived near the school.

EXERCISE **Now It's Your Turn (Part 1)**

If you were Ms. Smith, how would you handle this situation and why?

_____

_____

_____

_____

A PRINCIPAL'S DILEMMA (PART 2)

After ordering the students to calm down, Ms. Smith told Lamar to accompany her to her office. Although he kept insisting that he was innocent, Ms. Smith decided that she should investigate further. Therefore, she gave him a pat down by running her hands along his shoulders, back, buttocks, legs, and ankles. She found no sign of a cell phone. A few minutes later, a school custodian walked in and announced, "We found the phone!" It turned out that the cell phone had merely been misplaced.

EXERCISE **Now It's Your Turn (Part 2)**

1. If you were a 10-year-old child who had never gotten into trouble at school, how do you think you would feel if your schoolmates falsely accused you of stealing?

_____

_____

_____

_____

2. If you were a 10-year-old child who had never gotten into trouble at school, how do you think you would feel if your principal gave you a pat down?

_____

_____

_____

_____

3. In your opinion, what caused the principal to resort to a pat down rather than choosing another alternative?

_____

_____

_____

_____

4. In your opinion, how did the story end?

_____

_____

_____

_____

A PRINCIPAL'S DILEMMA (PART 3)

Later that day, when Lamar arrived home, his mother immediately noticed that something was wrong. When she asked how his day at school had gone, he said "Fine," but the boy seemed sullen and withdrawn. So she kept probing: "Are you sure that you had a good day?" When Lamar insisted that he had, his mother feared that her son had been bullied and was afraid to tell her. After she questioned him further, the child finally blurted out, "Ms. Smith was mean to me!" Upon hearing the full details, the parents became outraged.

When they voiced their displeasure to Ms. Smith, the principal downplayed the severity of their concerns and insisted that she had behaved appropriately. In reply to the parents' questions about why Ms. Smith had not bothered to telephone them or even send a note home about the incident, Ms. Smith indicated that they were overreacting. After all, she was an experienced school leader who had a good reputation. In the meantime, Lamar continued to exhibit signs of depression, which prompted his parents to seek professional counseling for him. Over time, tension between the parents and Ms. Smith increased, and the situation escalated to the point that the parents filed a civil lawsuit against Ms. Smith. In 2013, the case was broadcast on a nationally televised court show, and the judge ruled in the parents' favor: After reprimanding Ms. Smith, he ordered her to pay Lamar's counseling fees.

EXERCISE Now It's Your Turn (Part 3)

1. What are the most important messages that you learned from this story?

_____

_____

_____

_____

2. How can this story help you to become a more effective teacher of students of color?

_____

_____

_____

_____

CHAPTER HIGHLIGHTS

"A Principal's Dilemma" illustrates several important points:

- Being a school leader is not an easy job.
- Like K–12 teachers, school leaders can make decisions that can ameliorate or exacerbate race relations with parents and students of color.
- Just as most K–12 teachers have unaddressed mental baggage in the forms of stereotypes and negative beliefs about some students and parents of color, the same is true of many school leaders.

In fact, in the Mindset Study that I (Gail) described in *The Power of One: How You Can Help or Harm African American Students*, more than half of the educators indicated that most school principals do not even believe that African American students are capable of academic excellence.[1] Therefore, in this chapter, our goals are to help you better understand school leaders, to underscore the importance of strengthening your relations with them, and to help you realize that school leaders can become invaluable assets to you. Although the Teacher Confidence (TC) Study did not contain statements about school leaders, we will share additional research about school leaders and stories and strategies that can help you work well with them. Now, we'd like for you to examine your confidence level about school administrators by completing the next exercise.

EXERCISE   **Examining Your Self-Confidence About Working With School Leaders**

1. How confident are you about your ability to ask a White school leader for help and why?

_____

_____

_____

_____

2. How confident are you about your ability to ask an Asian American school leader for help and why?

_____

_____

_____

_____

3. How confident are you about your ability to ask a Latino school leader for help and why?

_____

_____

_____

_____

4. How confident are you about your ability to ask an African American school leader for help and why?

_____

_____

_____

_____

Some Basic Facts About School Principals

The following facts are from the National Center for Education Statistics:

- "During the 2011–12 school year, there were an estimated 115,540 principals of K–12 schools in the United States; 89,810 were public school principals."[2]

(Continued)

(Continued)

- "Among public school principals, 80 percent were non-Hispanic [W]hite, 10 percent were non-Hispanic [B]lack or African American, 7 percent were Hispanic, and 3 percent were another race or ethnicity."[3]

- "The percentage of public school principals who were female was 52 percent overall, 64 percent in primary schools, 42 percent in middle schools, 30 percent in high schools, and 40 percent in combined schools."[4]

- Approximately 62 percent of public school principals had a master's degree as their highest degree, and approximately 10 percent had a "doctorate/first professional degree."[5]

- "On average, public school principals spent 58.1 hours per week on all school-related activities, including 22.5 hours per week interacting with students."[6]

- "Public school principals had, on average, 7.2 years of experience as a principal, of which 4.2 years were spent in their current school."[7]

- "Public and private school principals reported having a major influence on decisions concerning evaluating teachers (96 and 84 percent, respectively), hiring new full-time teachers (85 and 86 percent, respectively), and setting discipline policy (80 and 82 percent, respectively)."[8]

WHY DEVELOPING STRONG PROFESSIONAL RELATIONSHIPS WITH SCHOOL LEADERS MATTERS

Although in this chapter we are mainly urging you to strive to develop a strong professional relationship with your school principal, we do want you to remember that doing so with all school leaders (including assistant principals, department chairs, literacy coaches, etc.) can make your job a lot easier. Principals and assistant principals may observe you teaching and write formal evaluations of your teaching efficacy. During your years as a beginning teacher, principals and assistant principals may be in a position to determine whether or not you are retained when budget cuts result in layoffs. Other school leaders can offer you teaching strategies, share resources, and help you solve specific teaching problems. One of the best ways that we can emphasize how you can benefit from forming strong, positive, professional relationships with school leaders—even across racial/ethnic lines—is to share another story with you. The following story is based on my (Rufus's) experiences with an outstanding school leader, who happened to be a middle-aged White male.

UP CLOSE AND PERSONAL: HOW I (RUFUS) BENEFITTED FROM THE EXPERTISE OF AN OUTSTANDING SCHOOL LEADER

Throughout my childhood and adolescence while growing up in Fontana, California, I always wanted to be a professional athlete, because I looked up to several famous athletes. During this time, I played on many children's and school sports teams. My hard work paid off because in 1978, I was drafted by and signed by the Minnesota Twins. I played "Single A" for one summer and then was released by the Minnesota Twins.

Being released devastated me, but it also forced me to return to college to finish my degree. During that time, I decided that I was going to earn a teaching credential, because I needed to let kids just like me—those who dreamed of having an athletic career—know that they needed a backup plan, in case their dream did not come true. But teaching was also a calling for me, for I had already been teaching Sunday School at my church for 12 years.

As the first African American male—and, for many years, the only African American teacher—at the middle school where I was hired, I worked hard in the classroom and focused on the individual student long before differentiated instruction became popular. In fact, Rand Shumway, the principal who hired me and who quickly became my mentor, emphasized differentiated learning back in the early 1980s. My individual goals targeted two groups: the quiet students and the athletes. I worked to challenge the high achievers and the low achievers as well.

If you are wondering whether or not my first years as a rookie teacher were easy, the answer is yes and no. My first two years were the hardest. Sometimes, I would go home around 8 p.m. because I coached school sports and needed to finish my lesson planning. Even after I arrived home, I would often work until early morning, developing lesson plans and thinking about the students who may not have done well on a previous lesson and the reasons why.

Although those first years were rough, on many occasions, having Mr. Shumway as my school principal definitely made them much easier. One way that he helped was to teach me how to deal with politics and bureaucracy associated with teaching. When these issues surfaced, Mr. Shumway advised me to close my classroom door and focus on the students' needs.

One of Mr. Shumway's most admirable qualities was his ability to diffuse potentially volatile racial conflicts. Later, when Mr. Shumway became principal of an elementary school in our district, White female teachers would send African American boys to his office as a result of misbehavior on many occasions. Mr. Shumway would usually ask the student to sit at a circular table outside of his office for several minutes. After the student had calmed down, Mr. Shumway would invite him into his office. Instead of belittling, scolding, or assuming that the boy was guilty, he would begin to ask the child questions about his interests, particularly about sports and his hobbies. If the boy said that he liked to play a particular sport, Mr. Shumway would continue to ask questions and segue into questions about whether or not the student liked and obeyed his coach.

During the period when I served as the district's technology coordinator, on the occasions when I was in Mr. Shumway's office at the time when a terrified African American boy came in, Mr. Shumway would introduce me to the child, tell the boy that I worked for the district, and then ask me to describe my sports background. Mr. Shumway used this method in order to establish trust with the student, diffuse tension, and help the child realize that even though the child didn't see any teachers who looked like him in his classroom, an African American male had a prominent position in the school district. By the time the meeting ended, Mr. Shumway had successfully helped the student understand that just as his sports team coach needed the team to work together, the same was true of his classroom teacher. He ended the meeting by telling the student to return to class, try to cooperate with his teacher, and return to Mr. Shumway's office the following day to summarize how his return to class had gone.

According to Mr. Shumway, 90 percent of the time, the student came back and said that everything had gone well in class. Mr. Shumway's humanistic approach infuriated a few teachers, especially those who believed that children should sit still and be quiet for most of the class session. However, his approach helped other teachers understand how their attitudes and classroom practices could actually create discipline problems. Consequently, some teachers realized that they could handle problematic behaviors on their own, without sending students to the office. As for me, Mr. Shumway's method taught me the importance of modifying discipline strategies to fit the particular student; the importance of being firm yet compassionate; and that in schools where there are few (if any) educators of color, through words and actions, a White school leader can set a tone that can have a far-reaching, positive effect on the school climate.

EXERCISE   What You Learned From "Up Close and Personal"

1. What are the most important messages that you learned from this story?

_____

_____

_____

_____

2. How can this story help you to become a more effective teacher of students of color?

_____

_____

_____

_____

CONCLUSION

Knowing how to work well with parents and your colleagues is important. The same is true of school leaders. In this chapter, we emphasized that regardless of their race or ethnicity, school principals and other school leaders can make your job a lot easier if you are able to form strong, positive, professional relationships with them. The following advice and strategies should move you closer to this goal.

ADVICE AND STRATEGIES

1. Understand with whom you are dealing.

Working with school leaders can be rewarding and challenging. Administrators are trained in specific areas of leadership. They have certain temperament and personality profiles that can be compatible or incompatible with yours. Therefore, understanding the type of leader with whom you are dealing is crucial.

For instance, some school principals know where they want the school to go and how they want the school run yet they allow teachers, staff, students, and parents to make decisions regarding that direction and vision. Eliciting the help from students, the community, and teachers creates buy-in. It also creates a sense of ownership. This results in lower school facility costs, for there is less damage to be repaired, and burglaries diminish when everyone is involved in the success of the school and thus the success of the students.

I (Rufus) actually experienced this in the school district where I spent my entire teaching career. To this day, there are no school security officers in those schools because of the involvement I mentioned earlier. The pulse of the community determined the success of the schools. During one period, when we (as a staff) started alienating the parents and students by implementing policies arbitrarily, we saw more damage to school property, negative changes in student behavior, and pushback from parents. As a classroom teacher, when you have the support of your principal and administration, you are empowered, and this will affect your morale and your teaching.

On the other hand, an administrator who is a manager with no vision will create and enforce a bunch of rules. Consequently, teachers, and students will find ways to circumvent the rules. I (Rufus) have also worked with this type of school leader. This leader is a strong disciplinarian who insists that the student handbook look like a guide to San Quentin or some other prison. Under his or her leadership, parents are dictated to and, in some cases, insulted and made to feel deficient because this type of school leader claims to be an expert on the behavior of all the students. As a result, school becomes more about controlling students and focusing on misbehavior rather than providing a powerful, enriching, challenging, and engaging curriculum that actually reduces discipline problems.

In contrast to the overly controlling school leader, the weak leader is ineffective and gets taken advantage of. Students have no respect for this type of leader, teachers have no respect for him or her, and the leader lacks self-respect. Additionally, this leader may appear to be distant and disconnected from students and school personnel, because the leader does not know how to fix the problems that his or her weak leadership style created. This type of school leader is the most dangerous because his or her leadership style results in low morale schoolwide.

Regardless of the type of school leader with whom you work, you can and should support the leader in a way that will enhance your ability to teach your students and to thrive in the workplace. If you are working with an administrator who does not accept recommendations well, then you must realize it early on or your workplace will become very tense. Therefore, it is vital to know when to limit your contact with a school leader and, if necessary, steer clear of the individual as much as possible. Negative, toxic, and demeaning school leaders can destroy your teaching self-confidence, undermine your efforts, and contribute to workplace unhappiness.

2. Invite school leaders to visit your classroom.

Inviting school leaders to observe a class activity or watch you teach a lesson is a good way to help them to better understand you and to see your teaching and classroom management strengths. I (Rufus) used to invite administrators into my classroom because I realized that although most school leaders went into teaching because they enjoyed teaching, their administrative duties often made it difficult for them to observe students engaged in actual learning activities. Therefore, inviting them into your classroom allows school leaders to return to their roots, where they can see some of the same students that they may have to discipline for misbehavior engaged in a learning activity. It also gives students an opportunity to shine and may give school leaders a different view of the students. Furthermore, it also allows you to get an informal observation that may strengthen your professional relationship with school leaders.

3. Be professional.

In order to earn respect from school leaders, you should always try to behave in a professional manner at work. The way in which you speak to school leaders, your colleagues, support staff, students, and parents will help school leaders form impressions of you, so make sure that they are the impressions that you desire. The way that you dress also matters. If you take your job seriously and want to be viewed as serious, competent, and professional, what you wear to work should reflect this. Wearing inappropriate clothing can send the wrong message to school leaders, parents, and students. Arriving at work on time, staying after school at least until the stipulated time to leave, preparing your lessons ahead of time and having them posted on the whiteboard or chalkboard, and making sure that students are engaged in some learning activity if and when a school leader unexpectedly visits your classroom all increase the likelihood that school leaders will view you and treat you in a professional manner.

4. Ask for help.

Good school leaders want their teachers to be successful because effective teachers improve the school's reputation and, thereby, the leaders' reputations. Therefore, if you need help, do not suffer in silence. For example, in Chapter 1, we explained that Michaela, a beginning teacher, was frustrated and overwhelmed after being told at the last minute that she would be teaching eleventh-grade English, which she had never taught before. Since the administration was responsible for unexpectedly giving her a new class, it would have been wise and appropriate for her to voice her concerns in a tactful way. If you find yourself in a similar predicament, let the school leader who is in charge of class schedules know that you appreciate his or her confidence in your abilities. Next, ask if the school leader can refer you to a teacher who has taught the course previously. Finally, ask what resources are available to help you prepare for the new course or class. Regardless of what you choose to say, the main point is to say something in person, by telephone, or by e-mail and to not be afraid to ask for help when you need it. When you ask, chances are that school leaders will reflect back to their years as beginning teachers, empathize with your situation, and provide you with assistance.

In the case where you have not been informed about what you will teach during the forthcoming academic year, you can use the following script as a template to organize your thoughts and what you want to say and then practice what you want to say ahead of time.

A Script to Use With School Leaders

(School leader's name):

I really want to do a good job this year, and I need your help. I would like to know if you will tell me classes (or grade level) I'll be teaching so that I can prepare my lesson plans in advance and locate resources that may help me.

---

5. Do your best to prepare for classroom observations.

Throughout the decades that I (Rufus) was a classroom teacher, I never became comfortable with formal classroom observations or unexpected visits from school leaders. Nevertheless, Ed Peltz, my first district superintendent, often brought dignitaries to visit my classroom. In fact, Mr. Peltz brought in two state superintendents of instruction and multiple county superintendents, state senators, and state congressional members.

The good news is that in the beginning, he usually warned me when he was planning to bring guests to my classroom (although over time, he would just pop in). So to reduce my anxiety, I would ask my principal, Rand Shumway, to do an informal observation first. Then, I would invite Mr. Peltz to come in and watch me teach. Mr. Peltz loved to visit classrooms! Asking Mr. Shumway and

Mr. Peltz to visit before the dignitaries came boosted my confidence and alleviated some of my anxiety. By the way, Mr. Peltz hated *F* grades. Although the school board directed him to implement a grading policy that included *F*s, his philosophy was that students do not earn *F*s; instead, because their education is *Incomplete*, teachers should give *I*s instead of *F*s. Consequently, because of his influence, I always felt like a failure when a student earned an *F* or an *I*. You should, too, because this mindset will help you strive harder to help students succeed academically.

6. Remember what you have in common.

Most school leaders are decent people who care dearly about what they are doing. Why would they spend most of their holidays, weekends, and evenings away from their families if they didn't? Furthermore, many were outstanding teachers before they became school leaders. If you keep these basic reminders in mind when you speak to, speak about, and interact with school leaders, it will enable you to treat them compassionately and to realize what you have in common. Also, keep in mind that as the instructional leader of your students, you have many duties and responsibilities. However, school leaders have to deal with much more than you do, and in most cases, you will never know the full extent of their work, why they make certain decisions, and why they behave as they do unless you have taken courses in administration or have a relative or friend who has that experience.

APPLYING WHAT YOU LEARNED TO YOUR *YES, I CAN!* JOURNAL

1. Summarize the most important points that you would like to remember from this chapter.

2. a. Identify a White school leader at your school site or at another school or the district office with whom you would like to form a stronger professional relationship.

   b. Ask the leader if you can meet with him or her to learn what he or she knows about working with students of color and parents of color, and ask for suggestions that can help you to strengthen your teaching and classroom management skills.

3. a. Identify an Asian American school leader at your school site or at another school or the district office with whom you would like to form a stronger professional relationship.

   b. Ask the leader if you can meet with him or her to learn what he or she knows about working with students of color and parents of color, and ask for suggestions that can help you to strengthen your teaching and classroom management skills.

4. a. Identify a Latino school leader at your school site or at another school or the district office with whom you would like to form a stronger professional relationship.

   b. Ask the leader if you can meet with him or her to learn what he or she knows about working with students of color and parents of color, and ask for suggestions that can help you to strengthen your teaching and classroom management skills.

5. a. Identify an African American school leader at your school site or at another school or the district office with whom you would like to form a stronger professional relationship.

   b. Ask the leader if you can meet with him or her to learn what he or she knows about working with students of color and parents of color, and ask for suggestions that can help you to strengthen your teaching and classroom management skills.

6. Read the following works and, in your journal, summarize the lessons/messages that can help you work more effectively with school leaders.

   • *Difficult Conversations: How to Discuss What Matters Most* by Douglas Stone, Bruce Patton, and Sheila Heen

   • *Resolving Conflicts at Work: A Complete Guide for Everyone on the Job* by Kenneth Cloke and Joan Goldsmith

   • *The Art of Leadership: A Practical Guide for People in Positions of Responsibility* by J. Donald Walters

   • *Lessons From High-Performing Hispanic Schools: Creating Learning Communities* edited by Pedro Reyes, Jay D. Scribner, and Alicia Paredes Scribner

Conclusion

Don't Throw in the Towel—How to Keep Going When You Feel Like Giving Up

In May 2013, Michaela, the second-year teacher to whom we introduced you in Chapter 1, celebrated two great milestones. The first was that she had finally finished the course work and exams to earn her master's degree. The second was that she had successfully completed her second year of teaching. Yes, it was true that her second year was challenging. That year, she had been assigned to teach eleventh graders for the first time. In spite of her best efforts, some students refused to cooperate and violated her class rules. In fact, things got so rough one day, she actually burst into tears in front of her students. Often, during that difficult second year, she had thought about quitting. Teaching was hard, and she doubted that she could make a long-term career out of this profession. She was sleep deprived most days because of the difficulties she experienced at work and the stress of staying on top of lesson planning and grading students' work combined with the requirements of her master's degree program. But Michaela not only hung in there and stayed the course, but she even received an outstanding teaching evaluation from her principal. In 2013, Michaela got a job at a high school in the same school district. This year, she was excited. She was more experienced, more confident, and certain that she would have a great year. She had done it and done it well. Now she was certain that yes, she could stay the course as a teacher and, over time, even become a mentor teacher or other school leader, and so can you.

If you remember the messages that we have shared throughout this book and apply the strategies,

- yes, you can have a rewarding teaching career;
- yes, you can work well with most students, including African American students and other students of color, low-income students, and struggling students; and

- yes, you can form strong, positive professional relations with your colleagues, parents, and school leaders.

We conclude with a list of confidence boosters.

Confidence Boosters

1. Start your morning with a moment of prayer or meditation to clear your mind; to improve your mood; to develop the right mindset about your job and your students, parents, colleagues, and school leaders; and to prepare to have a successful day.

2. Each day, speak positive affirmations about your purpose, ability to have a positive impact on students, and your ability to be an outstanding instructional leader.

3. When in doubt about how to act or handle a situation, treat all students—regardless of their race or ethnicity, gender, socioeconomic background, or academic level—in the way in which you would want your own biological child or other loved one to be treated.

4. Treat parents—regardless of their race or ethnicity, gender, English proficiency level, or socioeconomic background—in the way in which you would want to be treated.

5. Ask school leaders, colleagues, support staff, parents, and students for help when you need it.

6. Review your *Yes, I Can!* journal entries periodically to measure your professional growth and to identify areas on which you need to continue to work.

7. Be kind to and forgiving of yourself, and allow yourself to be human.

8. Seek to do your best but realize that perfection is an unattainable goal.

9. Don't magnify your mistakes or failures yet minimize your successes. Instead, learn what you can from your mistakes and celebrate each success, no matter how small it is.

10. Whenever you are having a bad day and wonder if you should quit, keep repeating to yourself, "Yes, I *can* work effectively with all of my students, including my African American, Latino, Asian American, biracial, and White students!" until your mood improves.

Appendix A

Background Information About the Teacher Confidence Study

In 2009, I (Gail) distributed the Teacher Confidence Study questionnaire that I created to four groups that attended professional development workshops that I conducted in California. One group consisted of 70 K–12 public school teachers in the Los Angeles Unified School District. The second group consisted of 57 K–12 teachers in a small northern California school district. The third group consisted of 72 teachers at a Catholic high school in northern California. The fourth group consisted of 94 teacher interns. The interns were prospective teachers who were enrolled in a teacher education program at a private university in southern California. Their prior teaching experience ranged from none to several years of substitute teaching. Within four months after they completed the questionnaire, each intern would be placed in a K–12 classroom as a first-year full-time teacher.

Appendix B

Demographic Information About the 293 Teacher Confidence Study Participants

1. How much teaching experience have you had in K–12 schools?

a. None	9.20%
b. One year or less	18.10%
c. 2–3 yrs.	11.30%
d. 4–5 yrs.	10.20%
e. More than 5 yrs.	49.80%

2. What grade level(s) do you teach?

a. Pre-K–3	10.90%
b. Grades 4–5	8.90%
c. Middle school	21.50%
d. High school	45.40%

3. What is your gender?

a. Male	31%
b. Female	67%

4. What is your race?

a. African American or Black	14%
b. Latino, Chicano, or Hispanic	14%
c. Asian American or Pacific Islander	10%
d. White, Anglo, or Caucasian	54%
e. Mixed race	1%

Note: Percentage totals that are less than 100 can be explained by the number of respondents who failed to answer a question.

Appendix C

Questionnaire Results From the 293 Teacher Confidence Study Participants

V = Very Confident   *S = Somewhat Confident*   *N = Not Confident*

1. How confident are you about your ability to treat all students fairly?

Total Sample:	V = 64%	S = 35%	N = 1%
Experienced Teachers:	V = 59%	S = 39%	N = 2%
Interns:	V = 73%	S = 26%	N = 1%

2. How confident are you about your classroom management skills?

Total Sample:	V = 43%	S = 53%	N = 3%
Experienced Teachers:	V = 54%	S = 43%	N = 3%
Interns:	V = 20%	S = 76%	N = 4%

3. How confident are you about your ability to effectively teach low-income students?

Total Sample:	V = 57%	S = 41%	N = 2%
Experienced Teachers:	V = 54%	S = 44%	N = 3%
Interns:	V = 64%	S = 35%	N = 1%

V = Very Confident   *S = Somewhat Confident*   *N = Not Confident*

4. How confident are you about your ability to effectively teach middle-class students?

Total Sample:	V = 69%	S = 28%	N = 2%
Experienced Teachers:	V = 68%	S = 29%	N = 3%
Interns:	V = 71%	S = 27%	N = 2%

5. How confident are you about your ability to effectively teach high-income students?

Total Sample:	V = 48%	S = 46%	N = 6%
Experienced Teachers:	V = 45%	S = 48%	N = 7%
Interns:	V = 54%	S = 43%	N = 3%

6. How confident are you about your ability to effectively teach high achievers?

Total Sample:	V = 55%	S = 41%	N = 3%
Experienced Teachers:	V = 48%	S = 47%	N = 4%
Interns:	V = 70%	S = 27%	N = 3%

7. How confident are you about your ability to effectively teach low achievers?

Total Sample:	V = 42%	S = 53%	N = 4%
Experienced Teachers:	V = 41%	S = 54%	N = 5%
Interns:	V = 45%	S = 52%	N = 2%

8. How confident are you about your ability to effectively teach students who read below grade level?

Total Sample:	V = 36%	S = 50%	N = 14%
Experienced Teachers:	V = 33%	S = 51%	N = 16%
Interns:	V = 43%	S = 47%	N = 10%

9. How confident are you about your ability to effectively teach students who have poor math skills?

Total Sample:	V = 40%	S = 42%	N = 13%
Experienced Teachers:	V = 35%	S = 42%	N = 16%
Interns:	V = 50%	S = 40%	N = 9%

V = Very Confident   *S = Somewhat Confident*   *N = Not Confident*

10. How confident are you about your ability to effectively teach girls?

Total Sample:	V = 79%	S = 21%	N = 0%
Experienced Teachers:	V = 77%	S = 23%	N = 0%
Interns:	V = 81%	S = 18%	N = 0%

11. How confident are you about your ability to effectively teach boys?

Total Sample:	V = 71%	S = 29%	N = 0%
Experienced Teachers:	V = 68%	S = 32%	N = 0%
Interns:	V = 77%	S = 23%	N = 0%

12. How confident are you about your ability to effectively teach White students?

Total Sample:	V = 70%	S = 29%	N = 1%
Experienced Teachers:	V = 67%	S = 32%	N = 1%
Interns:	V = 77%	S = 23%	N = 0%

13. How confident are you about your ability to effectively teach Asian American students?

Total Sample:	V = 67%	S = 33%	N = 0%
Experienced Teachers:	V = 63%	S = 36%	N = 1%
Interns:	V = 74%	S = 26%	N = 0%

14. How confident are you about your ability to effectively teach Latino students?

Total Sample:	V = 63%	S = 35%	N = 2%
Experienced Teachers:	V = 58%	S = 39%	N = 3%
Interns:	V = 73%	S = 26%	N = 1%

15. How confident are you about your ability to effectively teach African American females?

Total Sample:	V = 58%	S = 38%	N = 4%
Experienced Teachers:	V = 53%	S = 42%	N = 5%
Interns:	V = 69%	S = 31%	N = 0%

V = Very Confident   *S = Somewhat Confident*   *N = Not Confident*

16. How confident are you about your ability to effectively teach African American males?

Total Sample:	V = 55%	S = 40%	N = 5%
Experienced Teachers:	V = 50%	S = 43%	N = 7%
Interns:	V = 66%	S = 33%	N = 1%

17. How confident are you about incorporating racial issues into your lesson plans?

Total Sample:	V = 40%	S = 38%	N = 21%
Experienced Teachers:	V = 41%	S = 36%	N = 22%
Interns:	V = 38%	S = 43%	N = 19%

18. How confident are you about your ability to effectively address racial conflicts that may arise in your classroom?

Total Sample:	V = 40%	S = 45%	N = 14%
Experienced Teachers:	V = 39%	S = 45%	N = 15%
Interns:	V = 41%	S = 45%	N = 14%

19. How confident are you about your ability to work effectively with White parents?

Total Sample:	V = 59%	S = 38%	N = 3%
Experienced Teachers:	V = 56%	S = 40%	N = 4%
Interns:	V = 65%	S = 33%	N = 2%

20. How confident are you about your ability to work effectively with Asian American parents?

Total Sample:	V = 56%	S = 41%	N = 3%
Experienced Teachers:	V = 52%	S = 44%	N = 4%
Interns:	V = 64%	S = 35%	N = 1%

21. How confident are you about your ability to work effectively with Latino parents?

Total Sample:	V = 60%	S = 38%	N = 1%
Experienced Teachers:	V = 56%	S = 42%	N = 1%
Interns:	V = 68%	S = 30%	N = 2%

V = Very Confident   *S = Somewhat Confident*   *N = Not Confident*

22. How confident are you about your ability to work effectively with African American parents?

Total Sample:	V = 50%	S = 44%	N = 6%
Experienced Teachers:	V = 45%	S = 48%	N = 7%
Interns:	V = 60%	S = 36%	N = 3%

23. How confident are you about your ability to work effectively with parents who don't speak English?

Total Sample:	V = 26%	S = 44%	N = 28%
Experienced Teachers:	V = 26%	S = 41%	N = 31%
Interns:	V = 28%	S = 51%	N = 21%

Note: Percentage totals that are less than 100 can be explained by the number of respondents who failed to answer a question.

Notes

INTRODUCTION

1. MetLife. (2012). *The MetLife survey of the American teacher: Teachers, parents, and the economy.* New York, NY: Metropolitan Life Insurance Company.

CHAPTER 1

1. Thompson, G. L. (2007). *Up where we belong: Helping African American and Latino students rise in school and in life.* San Francisco, CA: Jossey Bass.
2. Thompson, G. L. (2010). *The power of one: How you can help or harm African American students.* Thousand Oaks, CA: Corwin.
3. Advancement Project. (2010, March). *Test, punish, and push out: How "Zero Tolerance" and high-stakes testing funnel youth into the school-to-prison pipeline.* Washington, DC: Advancement Project; Thompson, G. L. (2007). *Up where we belong: Helping African American and Latino students rise in school and in life.* San Francisco, CA: Jossey Bass.
4. Ogbu, J. U. (2003). *Black American students in an affluent suburb: A study of academic disengagement.* Mahwah, NJ: Lawrence Erlbaum Associates.
5. United States Census Bureau. (2011, September). *Income, poverty, and health insurance coverage in the United States: 2010.* Washington, DC: U.S. Government Printing Office.
6. The National Center on Family Homelessness. *The characteristics and needs of families experiencing homelessness.* Retrieved July 27, 2012 from http://www.familyhomelessness.org/media/306.pdf; p. 1.
7. Kunjufu, J. (2002). *Black students. Middle class teachers.* Chicago, IL: African American Images.
8. Kozol, J. (2005). *The shame of the nation: The restoration of apartheid schooling in America.* New York, NY: Crown Publishers; Thompson, G. L. (2007). *Up where we belong: Helping African American and Latino students rise in school and in life.* San Francisco, CA: Jossey Bass.
9. Ferguson, A. A. (2001). *Bad boys: Public schools in the making of Black masculinity.* Ann Arbor, MI: The University of Michigan Press; Hale, J. E. (2001). *Learning while Black: Creating educational excellence for African American children.* Baltimore, MD: John Hopkins University Press; Kunjufu, J. (2005). *Keeping Black boys out of special education.* Chicago, IL: African

American Images; Thompson, G. L. (2007). *Up where we belong: Helping African American and Latino students rise in school and in life.* San Francisco, CA: Jossey Bass.

10. Thompson, G. L. (2007). *Up where we belong: Helping African American and Latino students rise in school and in life.* San Francisco, CA: Jossey Bass; Thompson, G. L. (2010). *The power of one: How you can help or harm African American students.* Thousand Oaks, CA: Corwin.

CHAPTER 2

1. National Center for Education Statistics. (2012). *Racial/Ethnic enrollment in public schools (Indicator 6–2012).* Retrieved November 6, 2012 from http://nces.ed.gov/programs/coe/indicator_1er.asp

2. National Center for Education Statistics. (2012). *Participation in education. Elementary/Secondary enrollment. Table A-6–3.* Retrieved November 6, 2012 from http://nces.ed.gov/programs/coe/tables/table-1er-3.asp

3. National Center for Education Statistics. (2012). *Elementary and secondary education. school characteristics and climate. Table A-26–2.* Retrieved November 6, 2012 from http://nces.ed.gov/programs/coe/tables/table-rcp-2.asp

4. Thompson, G. L. (2007). *Up where we belong: Helping African American and Latino students rise in school and in life.* San Francisco, CA: Jossey Bass.

5. Ibid.

6. National Center for Education Statistics. (2012). *Racial/Ethnic enrollment in public schools (Indicator 6–2012).* Retrieved November 6, 2012 from http://nces.ed.gov/programs/coe/indicator_1er.asp

7. National Center for Education Statistics. (2012). *Participation in education. Elementary/Secondary enrollment. Table A-6–4.* Retrieved November 6, 2012 from http://nces.ed.gov/programs/coe/tables/table-1er-4.asp

8. Wing Sue, D. (2003). *Overcoming our racism: The journey to liberation.* San Francisco, CA: Jossey Bass, p. 38.

9. National Center for Education Statistics. (2012). *Participation in education. Elementary/Secondary enrollment. Table A-6–3.* Retrieved November 6, 2012 from http://nces.ed.gov/programs/coe/tables/table-1er-3.asp

10. Rasool, J. A., & Curtis, C. A. (2000). *Multicultural education in middle and secondary classrooms: Meeting the challenge of diversity and change.* Belmont, CA: Wadsworth/Thomson Learning.

11. Hein, J. (1995). *From Vietnam, Laos, and Cambodia: A refugee experience in the United States.* New York, NY: Twayne Publishers; Thompson, G. L. (1998). We didn't come here to be poor: The pre- and post-migration experiences of young immigrants. *Journal of Children & Poverty,* 5(1), 45–73.

12. National Center for Education Statistics. *Status and trends in the education of racial and ethnic minorities. Table 8.2b.* Retrieved November 14, 2012 from http://nces.ed.gov/pubs2010/2010015/tables/table_8_2b.asp

13. United States Census Bureau. (2011, March). Overview of race and Hispanic origin: 2010. *2010 census briefs.* U.S. Department of Commerce. Retrieved November 19, 2012 from www.census.gov/prod/cen2010/briefs/c2010br-02.pdf; p. 2.

14. U.S. Census Bureau News. (2011, March 24). *2010 census shows America's diversity*. U.S. Department of Commerce. Retrieved November 19, 2012 from http://www.census.gov/newsroom/releases/archives/2010_census/cb11-cn125.html; p.1.

15. National Center for Education Statistics. (2012). *Racial/ethnic enrollment in public schools (Indicator 6–2012)*. Retrieved November 6, 2012 from http://nces.ed.gov/programs/coe/indicator_1er.asp

16. National Center for Education Statistics. (2012). *Participation in education. Elementary/Secondary enrollment. Table A-6–3*. Retrieved November 6, 2012 from http://nces.ed.gov/programs/coe/tables/table-1er-3.asp

17. "Latinos' school success: Work in progress." (June 7, 2012). Executive Summary. *Education Week, 31*(34), 2.

18. Ibid.

19. National Center for Education Statistics. (2012). *Participation in education. Elementary/Secondary enrollment. Table A-6–4*. Retrieved November 6, 2012 from http://nces.ed.gov/programs/coe/tables/table-1er-4.asp

20. National Center for Education Statistics. (2012). *Racial/ethnic enrollment in public schools (Indicator 6–2012)*. Retrieved November 6, 2012 from http://nces.ed.gov/programs/coe/indicator_1er.asp

21. National Center for Education Statistics. (2012). *Participation in education. Elementary/Secondary enrollment. Table A-6–3*. Retrieved November 6, 2012 from http://nces.ed.gov/programs/coe/tables/table-1er-3.asp

22. National Center for Education Statistics. (2012). *Racial/ethnic enrollment in public schools (Indicator 6–2012)*. Retrieved November 6, 2012 from http://nces.ed.gov/programs/coe/indicator_1er.asp

23. Wing Sue, D. (2003). *Overcoming our racism: The journey to liberation*. San Francisco, CA: Jossey Bass.

24. Thompson, G. L. (2007). *Up where we belong: Helping African American and Latino students rise in school and in life*. San Francisco, CA: Jossey Bass.

25. Thompson, G. L. (2010). *The power of one: How you can help or harm African American students*. Thousand Oaks, CA: Corwin.

26. Ibid.

27. Thompson, G. L. (2000). What students say about bilingual education. *The Journal of At-Risk Issues, Winter/Spring*, 24–32; p. 27.

CHAPTER 3

1. West, C., & Ritz, D. (2009). *Brother West: Living and loving out loud. A memoir*. New York, NY: SmileyBooks, p. 10.

2. Ibid.

3. Ibid.

4. Ibid., 18.

5. Ibid.

6. Ibid.

7. Benard, B. (2004). *Resiliency: What we have learned*. San Francisco, CA: WestEd.

8. Thompson, G. L. (2007). *Up where we belong: Helping African American and Latino students rise in school and in life.* San Francisco, CA: Jossey Bass.

9. Wyner, J. S., Bridgeland, J. M., & Diiulio, J. Jr. (2007). *Achievement trap: How America is failing millions of high-achieving students from lower-income families.* Retrieved April 19, 2013 from http://www.civicenterprises.net/ Education; p. 10.

10. Ibid., 4.

11. Ibid., 6.

12. Ibid., 5–6.

13. Rochkind, J., Ott, A., Immerwahr, J., Doble, J., & Johnson, J. (2007). *Lessons learned: New teachers talk about their jobs, challenges and long-range plans.* Issue No. 1. Washington, DC National Comprehensive Center for Teacher Quality. Available at http://www.publicagenda.org/files/lessons_learned_1. pdf

14. Ibid., Issues No. 1, 2, & 3. Available at http://www.publicagenda.org/ media/lessons-learned-series-issue-no-1; http://www.publicagenda.org/ media/lessons-learned-series-issue-no-2; and http://www.publicagenda .org/media/lessons-learned-series-issue-no-3

15. Drew, D. E. (2011). *Stem the tide: Reforming science, technology, engineering, and math education in America.* Baltimore, MS: The Johns Hopkins University Press, p. 77.

16. Ibid., 92.

17. Bozeman Public Schools. *A parents' guide to Multi-tiered System of Support (MTSS).* Retrieved January 10, 2014 from http://www.bsd7.org/students_ parents/a_parent_s_guide_to_m_t_s_s; p. 1.

18. Ibid.

19. Ibid.

20. Thompson, G. L. (2000). What students say about bilingual education. *The Journal of At-Risk Issues,* Winter/Spring, 24–32; p. 27.

CHAPTER 4

1. Gonnerman, J. (2004). *Life on the outside: The prison odyssey of Elaine Bartlett.* New York, NY: Picador.

2. Ibid., 87.

3. Ibid.

4. Ibid.

5. Thompson, G. L. (2004). *Through ebony eyes: What teachers need to know but are afraid to ask about African American students.* San Francisco, CA: Jossey Bass.

6. Rochkind, J., Ott, A., Immerwahr, J., Doble, J., & Johnson, J. (2007). *Lessons learned: New teachers talk about their jobs, challenges and long-range plans.* Issue No. 2. Washington, DC National Comprehensive Center for Teacher Quality; p. 15. Available at http://www.publicagenda.org/media/lessons-learned-series-issue-no-2

7. National Center for Education Statistics. (2012). *Indicators of school crime and safety: 2011.* Washington, DC: Author, Table 12.3.

8. Ibid., Table 12.1.

9. Ibid., 14, 34.

10. Thompson, G. L. (2010). *The power of one: How you can help or harm African American students.* Thousand Oaks, CA: Corwin.

11. Ibid., 152.

12. Thompson, G. L. (2004). *Through ebony eyes: What teachers need to know but are afraid to ask about African American students.* San Francisco, CA: Jossey Bass.

13. Ibid.

14. De Becker, G. (1997). *The gift of fear: Survival signals that protect us from violence.* Boston, MA: Little, Brown, and Company; Thompson, G. L. (2000). What students say about bilingual education. *The Journal of At-Risk Issues, Winter/Spring,* 24–32; p. 27.

CHAPTER 5

1. Kaplan, D. A. (2013, January 14). "Bay Area medicine man." *Fortune,* pp. 81–86; p. 83.

2. Ibid.

3. Ibid., 93.

4. Rochkind, J., Ott, A., Immerwahr, J., Doble, J., & Johnson, J. (2007). *Lessons learned: New teachers talk about their jobs, challenges and long-range plans.* Issue No. 1. Washington, DC: National Comprehensive Center for Teacher Quality; p. 24. Available at http://www.publicagenda.org/media/lessons-learned-series-issue-no-1

5. Ibid.

6. Thompson, G. L. (2000). The real deal on bilingual education: Former language-minority students discuss effective and ineffective instructional practices. *Educational Horizons, Winter,* 128–140.

7. Ibid., 130.

8. Ibid.

9. Ibid., 131.

10. Ibid.

11. Ibid.

12. Ibid.

13. Ibid.

14. Ibid., 131–132.

15. Ibid., 132.

16. Ibid.

17. Ibid.

18. Ibid., 133.

19. Ibid.

20. Ibid., 134.

21. Ibid.

22. Ibid.

23. Thompson, G. L. (2000). What students say about bilingual education. *The Journal of At-Risk Issues, Winter/Spring,* 24–32; p. 27.

24. Ibid.

25. Council of Chief State School Officers. (2014). *The Common Core State Standards Initiative (CCSSI)*. Retrieved January 7, 2014 from http://www.ccsso.org/Resources/Programs/The_Common_Core_State_Standards_Initiative.html

26. Thompson, G. L. (2004). *Through ebony eyes: What teachers need to know but are afraid to ask about African American students.* San Francisco, CA: Jossey Bass.

27. Thompson, G. L. (2000). What students say about bilingual education. *The Journal of At-Risk Issues, Winter/Spring,* 24–32; p. 27.

CHAPTER 6

1. Thompson, G. L. (2000). What students say about bilingual education. *The Journal of At-Risk Issues, Winter/Spring,* 24–32; p. 27.

2. Ibid.

3. Thompson, G. L., & Louque, A. (2005). *Exposing the culture of arrogance in the academy: A blueprint for increasing Black faculty satisfaction.* Sterling, VA: Stylus, p. 106.

4. Ibid.

5. Ibid.

6. Ibid.

7. Thompson, G. L. (2010). *The power of one: How you can help or harm African American students.* Thousand Oaks, CA: Corwin, p. 42.

8. Ibid.

9. Thompson, G. L. (2007). *Up where we belong: Helping African American and Latino students rise in school and in life.* San Francisco, CA: Jossey Bass, p. 109.

10. Ibid., 106–107.

11. Ibid., 182.

12. Ibid., 43.

13. Ibid., 47.

14. Ibid.

15. Ibid., 48.

16. "Turnaround school Howe High examines professional development." (2013, March 1). *Indianapolis Recorder.* Retrieved July 3, 2013 from http://www.indianapolisrecorder.com/education/article_927ffeae-8275-11e2-b9b2-0019bb2963f4.html; p. 1.

17. Thompson, G. L. (2004). *Through ebony eyes: What teachers need to know but are afraid to ask about African American students.* San Francisco, CA: Jossey Bass.

18. Fischer, J., Garza, A., McClure, J., Dix, P., & Mokry, V. A. (2007). *A report of Spanish resources for mathematics teachers of English language learners.* San Marcos, TX: Department of Mathematics, Texas State University-San Marcos. Retrieved June 25, 2013 from http://gato-docs.its.txstate.edu/mathematics/mell/MELL-Documents/SpanishResources_Final_2007/Spanish%20Resources%20Final%202007.pdf

19. Thompson, G. L., & Louque, A. (2005). *Exposing the culture of arrogance in the academy: A blueprint for increasing Black faculty satisfaction.* Sterling, VA: Stylus, p. 149.

CHAPTER 7

1. Thompson, G. L. (1998). We didn't come here to be poor: The pre- and post-migration experiences of young immigrants. *Journal of Children & Poverty,* 5(1), 45–73.
2. Ibid.
3. U.S. Department of Education. (2005). *Parent and family involvement in education: 2002–03.* Washington, DC: National Center for Education Statistics.
4. Ibid.
5. Ibid.
6. U.S. Department of Education. (2001). *Efforts by public K–8 schools to involve parents in children's education: Do schools and parent reports agree?* Washington, DC: Office of Educational Research and Improvement.
7. U.S. Department of Education. (2001). *Family involvement in children's education: An idea book* (abridged version). Jessup, MD: Office of Educational Research and Improvement.
8. Mora, P. (2007). *How to reach out to parents of ELLs.* Retrieved July 25, 2013 from http://www.colorincolorado.org/educators/reachingout/outreach/
9. Willson, J. (n.d.). *How to communicate with non-English speaking parents.* Retrieved July 25, 2013 from http://www.ehow.com/how_7839963_communicate-nonenglish-speaking-parents.html
10. Breiseth, L., Robertson, K., & Lafond, S. (2011). *A guide for engaging ELL families: Twenty strategies for school leaders.* Retrieved July 25, 2013 from http://www.colorincolorado.org/principals/family

CHAPTER 8

1. National Center for Education Statistics. (2011). *Fast facts. Teacher trends.* Retrieved August 5, 2013 from http://nces.ed.gov/fastfacts/display.asp?id=28
2. Scholastic, & the Bill & Melinda Gates Foundation. (2012). *Primary sources 2012: America's teachers on the teaching profession.* Retrieved August 5, 2013 from http://www.scholastic.com/primarysources/pdfs/Gates2012_full.pdf; p. 59.
3. Ibid., 115.
4. The MetLife Survey of the American Teacher. (2010). *Collaborating for student success.* Retrieved from https://www.metlife.com/assets/cao/contributions/foundation/american-teacher/MetLife_Teacher_Survey_2009.pdf; p. 9.
5. Ibid.

6. Rochkind, J., Ott, A., Immerwahr, J., Doble, J., & Johnson, J. (2007). *Lessons learned: New teachers talk about their jobs, challenges and long-range plans.* Issue No. 1. Washington, DC National Comprehensive Center for Teacher Quality, p. 12. Available at http://www.publicagenda.org/media/lessons-learned-series-issue-no-1

7. CNN. (November 5, 2010). *Steve Perry interviews Arne Duncan on need for minority teachers.* Retrieved August 7, 2013 from http://premierespeakers.com/steve_perry/blog/2011/05/24/steve_perry_interviews_arne_duncan_on_need_for_minority_teachers

8. Boser, U. (2011). *Teacher diversity matters: A state-by-state analysis of teachers of color.* Retrieved August 13, 2013 from http://www.americanprogress.org/issues/education/report/2011/11/09/10657/teacher-diversity-matters/; p. 1.

CHAPTER 9

1. Thompson, G. L. (2010). *The power of one: How you can help or harm African American students.* Thousand Oaks, CA: Corwin, p. 165.

2. Bitterman, A., Goldring, R., & Gray, L. (2013). *Characteristics of public and private elementary and secondary school principals in the United States: Results from the 2011–12 Schools and Staffing Survey (NCES 2013–313).* U.S. Department of Education. Washington, DC: National Center for Education Statistics. Retrieved March 10, 2013 from http://nces.ed.gov/pubs2013/2013313.pdf

3. Ibid., 3.

4. Ibid.

5. Ibid., 4.

6. Ibid., 5.

7. Ibid., 6.

8. Ibid., 7.

Index

CORWIN

A SAGE Company

The Corwin logo—a raven striding across an open book—represents the union of courage and learning. Corwin is committed to improving education for all learners by publishing books and other professional development resources for those serving the field of PreK–12 education. By providing practical, hands-on materials, Corwin continues to carry out the promise of its motto: **"Helping Educators Do Their Work Better."**